GREEK IS

Travel Guide

The Citi-scaper

Table of Contents

Introduction

The Greek Islands are a magical and enchanting destination, offering visitors a perfect combination of stunning landscapes, crystal-clear waters, and rich cultural heritage. This travel guide is the ultimate handbook for anyone planning a trip to the Greek Islands.

The guidebook provides comprehensive coverage of all the islands, from the popular tourist hotspots to the hidden gems waiting to be discovered. It offers detailed information on each island's history, culture, and cuisine, as well as practical tips on accommodation, transportation, and activities.

The book is divided into chapters, each one dedicated to useful information on getting around, where to eat, and what to see and do. The guidebook also features a comprehensive section on the Greek language, offering readers useful phrases and expressions to enhance their experience of the islands.

This travel guide to the Greek Islands is an essential resource for anyone looking to make the most of their trip. With its comprehensive coverage, detailed information, and insider tips, this guidebook is the perfect companion for any traveler to the Greek Islands.

Chapter 1

Overview

The Greek Islands are a stunning collection of over 2000 islands, each offering a unique and enchanting experience to travelers. From the bustling tourist hotspots to the quiet, undiscovered gems, the Greek Islands are a must-visit destination for any traveler seeking beauty, culture, and adventure.

The islands are located in the Aegean and Ionian Seas, and they are divided into several groups, each with its own distinct character and charm. The most popular island groups are the Cyclades, the Dodecanese, the Ionian Islands, and the Sporades.

The Cyclades, which include Santorini, Mykonos, and Paros, are known for their stunning white-washed buildings, blue-domed churches, and turquoise waters. These islands are a perfect destination for those seeking a lively nightlife, picturesque villages, and delicious Mediterranean cuisine.

The Dodecanese islands, including Rhodes, Kos, and Patmos, are known for their rich history and archaeological sites. The island of Rhodes, in particular, is home to the impressive Medieval City of Rhodes, a UNESCO World Heritage Site.

The Ionian Islands, including Corfu, Zakynthos, and Kefalonia, are lush and green, with stunning beaches and crystal-clear waters. These islands are perfect for those seeking a more laid-back, relaxed atmosphere, with charming villages, friendly locals, and plenty of opportunities for outdoor activities.

The Sporades islands, including Skiathos and Skopelos, are less developed and offer a more tranquil and secluded atmosphere. These islands are perfect for those seeking a peaceful escape, with stunning beaches, unspoiled natural beauty, and delicious local cuisine.

One of the unique features of the Greek Islands is the concept of "filoxenia," which translates to "hospitality." The locals on the islands take great pride in welcoming visitors and making them feel at home. Whether you're staying in a small family-run guesthouse or a luxury resort, you'll be treated like family and experience the warmth and generosity of the Greek people.

Another feature that sets the Greek Islands apart is the delicious food. Fresh seafood, grilled meats, and fresh vegetables are the staples of Greek cuisine, and each island has unique dishes and specialties. Whether you're enjoying a traditional Greek salad, sipping on a glass of ouzo, or indulging in a slice of baklava, you'll be treated to an explosion of flavor and taste.

In summary, the Greek Islands are a magical and captivating destination, offering a unique blend of history, culture, natural beauty, and hospitality. With so much to see and do, from exploring ancient ruins to lounging on pristine beaches, the Greek Islands are the perfect travel destination for anyone seeking a memorable and enriching experience.

History

The Greek islands are a cluster of over 6,000 islands and islets, of which only a few hundred are inhabited. These islands are located in the Aegean and Ionian Seas and are known for their rich history. The history of the Greek islands is as fascinating as the islands themselves.

The Greek islands have a long and complex history that dates back to ancient times. The islands played a significant role in the development of the Greek civilization and were the center of the Mediterranean world. The ancient Greeks were great seafarers and traders, and the islands provided them with a strategic advantage in terms of trade and communication.

The earliest known civilization on the Greek islands was the Minoan civilization, which flourished on the island of Crete from around 2700 BC to 1450 BC. The Minoans were a highly advanced civilization, known for their intricate art, architecture, and writing systems. They also had a sophisticated maritime trade network, which extended throughout the Mediterranean and beyond.

In the centuries that followed, the Greek islands were occupied by a succession of invaders, including the Mycenaeans, Persians, Romans, and Byzantines. Each of these civilizations left its mark on the islands, influencing their culture, architecture, and way of life.

The Greek islands played a pivotal role in the development of Christianity. Many of the islands, including Patmos and Hydra, are associated with early Christian saints and the apostles. The island of Patmos is particularly significant as it is believed to be the place where St. John wrote the Book of Revelation.

During the Ottoman era, the Greek islands were occupied by the Ottoman Empire and remained so until the early 19th century. The Ottoman occupation had a profound impact on the islands, shaping their culture, language, and customs. Many of the islands also played a crucial role in the Greek War of Independence, which led to the establishment of the modern Greek state in 1832.

Today, the Greek islands are a popular tourist destination. The islands' unique blend of ancient history, natural beauty, and modern amenities makes them an ideal vacation spot. The islanders are known for their hospitality and warmth, and visitors can experience the traditional Greek way of life in the islands' picturesque villages and towns.

The history of the Greek islands is a rich and fascinating story that spans thousands of years. From the ancient Minoans to the modern-day tourist industry, the islands have played a vital role in shaping the culture and civilization of Greece. The islands' history is an essential part of their charm and allure, and visitors to the islands can immerse themselves in this rich history while enjoying the islands' natural beauty and modern amenities.

Climate

Greece is renowned for its stunning islands that attract millions of visitors every year. Each island boasts its distinct charm, but they all share an exceptional Mediterranean climate. The Greek islands enjoy hot and dry summers, as well as mild and rainy winters, typical of a Mediterranean climate.

The islands are situated in the southeastern region of Europe, which means they experience a lot of sunshine throughout the year. The summers are long, with hot and dry weather that extends from June to September, and the winters are mild with occasional rains from October to May.

The warm and dry summers make the Greek islands the perfect destination for those who love the sun, sea, and sand. The daytime temperatures can soar up to 40°C (104°F), so it's essential to stay hydrated and wear light clothing. The sea temperature is also perfect for swimming, making it an excellent way to cool off during the hot afternoons.

During the summer, the islands come alive with festivals, markets, and street parties. The locals celebrate their traditions, culture, and religion in a way that is unique to each island. It's a great time to experience the island's way of life and mingle with the locals.

In contrast, the mild winters are a great time to explore the island's historical sites, museums, and monuments. The temperatures rarely drop below 10°C (50°F), which makes it a pleasant time to walk around and discover the island's hidden gems. Many restaurants and cafes are also open during the winter, providing an excellent opportunity to try out the local cuisine.

If you're planning to stay on one of the islands for an extended period, it's worth noting that the Mediterranean climate can have an impact on your home. For example, the warm summers can cause cracks in the walls, and the salty air can corrode metal fixtures.

However, many homes are built to withstand the climate, and it's a good idea to seek advice from a local builder or architect when planning to buy or build a home on one of the islands.

The climate of the Greek islands is a perfect blend of warm and dry summers and mild, rainy winters. The weather creates an ideal environment for those who love to soak up the sun, swim in the sea, and explore the islands. Whether you're looking to relax on the beach or immerse yourself in the island's culture, the Greek islands offer something for everyone.

Why Visit?

The Greek Islands are a mesmerizing group of islands located in the Aegean and Ionian Seas that offer some of the most stunning and unforgettable experiences one can have while traveling. Each of these islands has its unique identity, rich cultural heritage, and breathtaking natural beauty.

With their clear waters, golden sand beaches, ancient ruins, and charming white-washed villages, the Greek Islands have become a popular tourist destination, and for good reason.

If you're looking for a place to escape the stresses of modern life, then the Greek Islands are the perfect destination. The laid-back lifestyle, warm hospitality, and relaxed atmosphere of the islands will immediately put you at ease. Whether you're looking to soak up the sun on the beach, explore ancient ruins, or simply take a leisurely stroll through the narrow cobblestone streets of a picturesque village, there is something for everyone.

One of the main reasons to visit the Greek Islands is their incredible beauty. The islands boast a diverse range of landscapes, from the rugged mountain ranges of Crete to the lush green forests of Corfu, and everything in between.

The azure waters of the Aegean and Ionian Seas, dotted with charming fishing villages and secluded coves, are truly a sight to behold. Imagine waking up to the sound of the waves lapping at the shore, breathing in the fresh sea air, and watching the sunrise over the horizon - this is the kind of experience that the Greek Islands offer.

In addition to their natural beauty, the Greek Islands are also steeped in history and culture. The islands are home to some of the world's most significant archaeological sites, such as the ancient city of Knossos on Crete and the Acropolis in Athens. These sites offer a glimpse into the rich history of the Greek people, who have left an indelible mark on the world through their art, literature, philosophy, and more. For those interested in learning more about Greek culture, there is no better place to visit than the islands.

Another reason to visit the Greek Islands is the food. Greek cuisine is renowned for its fresh, healthy ingredients and bold flavors. From fresh seafood to mouth-watering meze dishes, there is something to tantalize every taste bud. Imagine sitting on a terrace overlooking the sea, savoring a plate of grilled octopus, or enjoying a glass of crisp white wine while watching the sunset - these are the kinds of experiences that make the Greek Islands so special.

Finally, the Greek Islands offer the chance to escape the hustle and bustle of modern life and experience a simpler, more relaxed way of living. The locals are friendly and welcoming, and the pace of life is much slower than in other parts of the world. You'll have the chance to connect with nature, reflect on life, and simply be present in the moment - something that we all need from time to time.

The Greek Islands are a truly magical destination that offer something for everyone. Whether you're looking for natural beauty, history and culture, delicious food, or simply a chance to unwind, the islands will not disappoint.

Best Time to Visit

The best time to visit the Greek Islands is largely dependent on what you're looking for in a vacation. Each season offers its unique charm, and the best time to visit will depend on your preferences, budget, and travel goals.

The high season for tourism in the Greek Islands is typically from mid-June to mid-September, during the summer months when the weather is hot and sunny, and the waters are perfect for swimming. This is the peak season for tourism, and the islands can get crowded and expensive during this time. However, if you're looking for a lively atmosphere, vibrant nightlife, and a chance to soak up the sun, then this is the best time to visit.

If you prefer to avoid the crowds and high prices, then it's best to visit the Greek Islands in the shoulder season, which is from April to early June and from mid-September to October. During this time, the weather is still warm and pleasant, and the crowds have yet to arrive or have already left. The sea is also warmer in September and October, making it perfect for swimming.

If you're looking to save money and don't mind cooler temperatures, then visiting the Greek Islands in the low season, which is from November to March, can be a great option. During this time, you'll find fewer tourists and lower prices on accommodation, flights, and activities. The weather can be unpredictable, and some businesses may be closed, but you'll still be able to experience the natural beauty and charm of the islands without the crowds.

It's worth noting that some of the smaller islands may have limited facilities or transportation options during the low and shoulder seasons, so it's best to do your research and plan accordingly. Ultimately, the best time to visit the Greek Islands depends on your personal preferences and what you're looking to get out of your vacation.

Chapter 2

Planning Your Trip

Planning a trip to the Greek Islands can be an exciting and fulfilling experience. With so many islands to choose from, each offering its unique charm and beauty, there's no shortage of options for travelers seeking a memorable vacation. However, planning your trip can also be overwhelming, particularly if you're not familiar with the islands or Greece as a whole.

The key to a successful trip to the Greek Islands is careful planning and research. From choosing the best time to visit to deciding on which islands to include in your itinerary, there are many factors to consider when planning your trip. In this chapter, we'll guide you through the planning process, providing you with the essential information you need to create the perfect Greek Islands vacation.

Visa Requirements

Visiting the Greek Islands can be an incredibly rewarding experience for travelers looking for sun, sea, and adventure. However, before packing your bags and jetting off, it's important to know about the visa requirements for entry into Greece.

Fortunately, for many travelers, Greece is a member of the European Union, which means that citizens of most EU countries can enter Greece without a visa. Additionally, citizens of countries such as the United States, Canada, and Australia can enter Greece for up to 90 days without a visa for tourism purposes.

However, it's essential to check with your country's embassy or consulate to ensure that you are eligible to enter Greece without a visa. Some countries may require their citizens to obtain a visa or permit to enter Greece, especially if you plan to stay for an extended period.

For instance, if you are planning to work or study in Greece, you will need to obtain a visa. Suppose you are traveling with children, including infants and minors. In that case, you may need to provide additional documentation, such as birth certificates or parental consent letters, to prove that you have legal custody of the child.

Another essential aspect to consider is the validity of your passport. Your passport should be valid for at least six months beyond your intended stay in Greece. Suppose your passport is set to expire soon. In that case, it's recommended that you renew it before traveling to avoid any issues with customs and border control.

It's also vital to note that due to the ongoing COVID-19 pandemic, travel restrictions and requirements can change at any time. It's essential to stay updated on the latest travel advisories and requirements for entry into Greece, such as presenting a negative COVID-19 test result or proof of vaccination.

In summary, researching and understanding the visa requirements for Greece is crucial to ensure a smooth and stress-free travel experience. Whether you're a seasoned traveler or a first-time adventurer, taking the time to plan and prepare for your trip will guarantee that you have an unforgettable experience exploring the stunning Greek Islands.

Travel Insurance

When it comes to planning a trip to the Greek Islands, there are a few important things to consider, and one of the most critical is travel insurance. Travel insurance is a type of insurance that can protect you from unexpected events that can occur while you're traveling, such as trip cancellations, medical emergencies, lost or stolen luggage, and more. It's essential to have travel insurance in case of an emergency, as it can provide you with peace of mind and financial protection.

There are various types of travel insurance policies available, so it's crucial to choose the one that best fits your needs. For example, if you're planning to engage in adventurous activities like hiking or water sports, you may need a policy that includes coverage for these activities. If you're traveling with expensive equipment like a camera or laptop, you may want to consider a policy that includes coverage for lost or stolen items.

One example of a comprehensive travel insurance policy is the "Allianz Global Assistance Classic Plan." This plan includes coverage for trip cancellation and interruption, emergency medical and dental expenses, baggage loss and delay, and more. It also offers 24/7 assistance services, including emergency medical transportation and assistance with replacing lost travel documents.

Another example is the "World Nomads Explorer Plan," which offers coverage for a wide range of adventurous activities, including bungee jumping, scuba diving, and skiing. It also includes coverage for emergency medical and dental expenses, trip cancellation and interruption, and more. This plan is designed for travelers who want to engage in adventurous activities and need comprehensive coverage for unexpected events.

When choosing a travel insurance policy, it's essential to read the policy details carefully to understand what's included and what's not. Some policies may have exclusions or limitations that you need to be aware of. It's also important to compare policies from different providers to find the one that best fits your needs and budget.

Travel insurance is a critical part of planning your trip to the Greek Islands. It can provide you with financial protection and peace of mind in case of unexpected events. Take the time to research and compare different policies to find the one that best fits your needs, and make sure to read the policy details carefully to understand what's included and what's not. With the right travel insurance policy in place, you can enjoy your trip to the Greek Islands with confidence.

Budgeting for Your Trip

Budgeting for your trip is an important step in planning your travel to the Greek Islands. Whether you're a budget traveler or looking for a luxurious vacation, it's essential to plan your expenses and stick to a budget to ensure you don't overspend.

The first step in budgeting for your trip is to determine your total budget. This should include all of your expenses, including airfare, accommodations, transportation, food, activities, and souvenirs. Once you've determined your total budget, you can start breaking down your expenses into categories.

Airfare and accommodations are usually the most significant expenses when traveling to the Greek Islands. You can save money on airfare by booking your flights in advance, comparing prices from different airlines, and considering alternate airports. For accommodations, there are various options, including hotels, hostels, and vacation rentals. Hostels are often the most budget-friendly option, while vacation rentals can be a more cost-effective option if you're traveling with a group or family.

Transportation is another significant expense to consider when budgeting for your trip. If you plan to explore multiple islands, you may need to take ferries or other forms of transportation, which can add up quickly. To save money, consider purchasing a multi-day ferry pass or renting a car if you're comfortable driving on the islands.

Food and drinks can also be a significant expense, especially if you plan to eat out at restaurants. To save money, consider cooking some of your meals or purchasing groceries at local markets. You can also try traditional street food, which is often cheaper and can give you a taste of local cuisine.

Activities and tours can be a fun way to explore the Greek Islands, but they can also add up quickly. To save money, consider doing free activities, such as hiking or visiting public beaches. You can also look for discounts on tours and activities or consider traveling during the shoulder season when prices are lower.

Finally, don't forget to budget for souvenirs and gifts. It's easy to overspend on souvenirs, so consider setting a limit or only purchasing items that are meaningful or unique to the Greek Islands.

Budgeting for your trip to the Greek Islands is essential to ensure you don't overspend and can enjoy your vacation without worrying about finances. Take the time to plan your expenses and stick to your budget, and you'll be able to make the most of your trip without breaking the bank.

Chapter 3

Transportation Options

Transportation is a critical aspect of travel, and when it comes to exploring the Greek Islands, there are various options available. From ferries to buses, taxis, and rental cars, there are different modes of transportation that you can choose depending on your budget, itinerary, and travel style.

Each transportation option has its advantages and disadvantages, and it's essential to consider these factors before making your decision. For example, ferries are an excellent option for island hopping and offer stunning views of the Aegean Sea, but they can be time-consuming and may not be the most comfortable option for those prone to seasickness. Rental cars offer more flexibility and convenience, but they can be expensive and challenging to navigate on narrow, winding island roads.

In this chapter, we'll explore the different transportation options available in the Greek Islands, their pros and cons, and tips for choosing the right option for your trip. Whether you're a budget traveler or looking for a more luxurious experience, there's a transportation option that can fit your needs and help you make the most of your trip.

Let's dive in and explore the transportation options available in the Greek Islands.

Getting There

Getting to the Greek Islands is an essential part of any travel experience in Greece. There are various transportation options available, and choosing the right one can make your trip much more enjoyable. Here, we'll explore the different ways to get to the Greek Islands and provide you with the information required to make an informed decision.

By Air

Flying to the Greek Islands is the most convenient and popular mode of transport. Greece has 27 airports, with Athens International Airport being the largest and busiest. From Athens, you can catch a connecting flight to the islands. Most Greek Islands have their own airport, so flying directly to your destination is possible.

Some of the most popular airlines that offer flights to the Greek Islands are Aegean Airlines, Olympic Air, Ryanair, and EasyJet. The flight time from Athens to the islands is usually less than an hour, making it a quick and easy option.

By Sea

Taking a ferry to the Greek Islands is a popular option among travelers, as it allows you to enjoy the beautiful scenery along the way. Greece has a vast network of ferries that connect the islands to the mainland and each other. Ferry schedules can vary depending on the season, so it's best to check before booking.

There are various types of ferries available, ranging from high-speed catamarans to slower, more traditional ferries. The high-speed ferries are faster and more expensive, while the slower ferries are cheaper and provide a more leisurely journey. You can purchase ferry tickets online or at the port before departure.

By Car

If you're planning on exploring more than one island, renting a car is a great option. Most of the Greek Islands have car rental companies, and the process of renting a car is straightforward. However, keep in mind that some islands have narrow and winding roads, so driving can be challenging.

It's also possible to take your car on the ferry to the islands. Some ferries allow cars to be transported, and it's a convenient option if you're traveling with a group or have a lot of luggage.

By Bus

If you're on a budget, taking a bus to the Greek Islands is a great option. Buses operate from Athens to most of the islands, and the prices are reasonable. However, keep in mind that the journey can be long and tiring, so it's best to bring some snacks and entertainment.

Getting to the Greek Islands is an adventure in itself. Whether you choose to fly, take the ferry, rent a car, or take the bus, you'll be treated to stunning views and a unique travel experience. Make sure to choose the transportation option that best suits your budget and travel style, and don't forget to check schedules and book in advance to avoid any last-minute stress.

Getting Around

Once you arrive at the Greek Islands, you'll need to figure out how to get around. Luckily, there are various transportation options available to help you explore the islands.

Ferries

Ferries are the most common and convenient mode of transportation for island hopping. Greece has an extensive ferry network that connects the islands to each other and the mainland. There are two types of ferries: high-speed and conventional.

High-speed ferries, also known as catamarans, are faster and more expensive. They're a great option if you're short on time or want to travel in comfort. However, they can be crowded during peak season, and it's best to book in advance.

Conventional ferries are slower but more affordable. They're a popular option among backpackers and budget travelers. Most ferries have indoor and outdoor seating areas, as well as cafes and shops.

Domestic Flights

If you're traveling long distances, taking a domestic flight is a great option. Greece has several airports, and most islands have their own airport. The most popular airlines that offer domestic flights are Aegean Airlines, Olympic Air, and Sky Express. However, keep in mind that flights can be expensive during peak season, and it's best to book in advance.

Buses and Taxis

If you're staying in one place and want to explore the local area, taking a bus or taxi is a good option. Buses are affordable and operate regularly, but they can be crowded during peak season. Taxis are more expensive but offer a more comfortable and convenient ride. Make sure to agree on a price before getting in the taxi to avoid any surprises.

Car and Scooter Rentals

Renting a car or scooter is a great way to explore the islands at your own pace. Most islands have car rental companies, and the process is straightforward. However, keep in mind that some islands have narrow and winding roads, so driving can be challenging. Scooters are a popular option among backpackers and budget travelers, but make sure to wear a helmet and drive safely.

Getting around the Greek Islands is an adventure in itself. Whether you choose to take a ferry, fly, take a bus or taxi, or rent a car or scooter, you'll be treated to stunning views and a unique travel experience. Make sure to choose the transportation option that best suits your budget and travel style, and don't forget to check schedules and book in advance to avoid any last-minute stress.

Chapter 4

Accommodation Options

When planning a trip to the Greek Islands, choosing the right accommodation is an important part of the process. With a wide range of options to suit different budgets and preferences, it's important to consider all of your choices before making a decision.

In this chapter, we will focus on one of the most popular accommodation options in the Greek Islands: hotels. Whether you're looking for a luxurious beachfront resort, a comfortable mid-range hotel in the heart of town, or a budget-friendly option for backpackers, there is a hotel for every type of traveler.

We will explore the different types of hotels available, as well as some of the most popular hotels in the Greek Islands. We will also provide tips for booking your hotel and making the most of your stay.

So, whether you're planning a romantic getaway, a family getaway, or a solo trip, read on to discover everything you need to know about hotels in the Greek Islands.

Hotels

When it comes to accommodation options in the Greek Islands, hotels are a popular choice for many travelers. With a wide range of options to suit different budgets and preferences, there is a hotel for every type of traveler in the Greek Islands.

One of the most popular hotel options in the Greek Islands are luxury hotels, which offer guests the ultimate in comfort and relaxation. Many of these hotels are located right on the beach, with stunning views of the Aegean Sea. Some examples of luxury hotels in the Greek Islands include the Mykonos Grand Hotel & Resort, the Grace Santorini, and the Domes of Elounda in Crete.

For those who are looking for a more affordable option, there are plenty of mid-range hotels that offer comfortable accommodations without breaking the bank. Many of these hotels are situated in the heart of the island's main town, making it easy to explore all the local attractions. Some popular mid-range hotels in the Greek Islands include the Anemomilos Hotel in Santorini, the Aegean Sky Hotel in Rhodes, and the Zante Maris Suites in Zakynthos.

If you're traveling on a tight budget, there are also plenty of budget-friendly hotels in the Greek Islands. These hotels may not offer the same level of luxury as the more expensive options, but they provide a comfortable and convenient base for exploring the island. Some examples of budget-friendly hotels in the Greek Islands include the Paros Bay Hotel in Paros, the Golden Sun Hotel in Mykonos, and the Captain's Hotel in Zakynthos.

No matter what type of hotel you choose, you can expect warm hospitality, friendly service, and delicious local cuisine. Many hotels also offer a range of amenities, such as swimming pools, spas, and fitness centers, to help you make the most of your stay.

When booking your hotel in the Greek Islands, it's important to consider your travel dates and the location of the hotel. During peak season, hotels can book up quickly, so it's best to book in advance to secure your preferred accommodations. Additionally, if you're planning to explore the island, you may want to choose a hotel that's located near public transportation or within walking distance of local attractions.

Overall, hotels in the Greek Islands offer travelers a comfortable and convenient base for exploring the beauty and charm of these stunning islands. With so many options to choose from, you're sure to find the perfect hotel to suit your budget and preferences.

Booking a hotel in the Greek Islands can be an exciting part of your travel planning process. Here are some tips to help you navigate the booking process and ensure that you find the best hotel for your needs:

Start your search early: As mentioned earlier, hotels in the Greek Islands can book up quickly during peak season. To avoid disappointment, start your search early and book your hotel well in advance.

Use online booking platforms: There are many online booking platforms available that allow you to compare prices and amenities across a wide range of hotels. Some popular platforms include Booking.com, Expedia, and Hotels.com.

Read reviews: Before you book a hotel, be sure to read reviews from other travelers. This can help you get a sense of the hotel's quality and any potential issues you may encounter during your stay.

Consider location: As mentioned earlier, the location of your hotel can have a big impact on your overall experience. Consider what activities you want to do and choose a hotel that's conveniently located near those attractions.

Look for deals and discounts: Many hotels offer deals and discounts for early bookings, extended stays, or other promotions. Keep an eye out for these offers to save money on your hotel stay.

Check cancellation policies: It's always a good idea to check a hotel's cancellation policy before booking, in case your plans change or unforeseen circumstances arise.

Contact the hotel directly: If you have specific questions or requests, consider contacting the hotel directly to see if they can accommodate your needs.

By following these tips, you can make the booking process a breeze and find the perfect hotel for your Greek Islands adventure.

Villas and Apartments

One popular option that offers a great balance of comfort, convenience, and affordability are villas and apartments.

Villas and apartments are ideal for travelers who prefer a more private and spacious living arrangement. These properties offer a home away from home, with plenty of space to relax, unwind and enjoy your surroundings. They also provide ample opportunities to cook your own meals, which can be a great way to save money and explore local flavors.

When it comes to choosing a villa or apartment, there are a few key things to keep in mind. Firstly, consider the location. Do you want to be close to the beach or in a quiet residential area? Would you prefer to be in the heart of the action or away from the crowds? Think about what matters most to you and choose a property that fits your preferences.

Another important consideration is the size of the property. Villas and apartments come in a variety of sizes, from cozy one-bedroom apartments to sprawling five-bedroom villas. Consider the size of your group and the type of experience you're looking for when choosing a property.

Of course, amenities are also an important consideration when choosing a villa or apartment. Look for properties that offer the amenities that matter most to you, whether that's a private pool, air conditioning, Wi-Fi, or a fully equipped kitchen.

There are many great options for villas and apartments across the Greek Islands. Here are a few examples:

The Villa Nafsika in Crete is a stunning four-bedroom villa with a private pool and breathtaking sea views. This property offers plenty of space and luxury, making it ideal for groups of friends or families.

For a more budget-friendly option, the Sea Breeze Apartments in Santorini offer clean and comfortable accommodations at an affordable price. These apartments are just steps away from the beach and offer stunning views of the Aegean Sea.

If you're looking for a truly unique experience, consider staying at the Windmill Villas in Mykonos. These traditional windmills have been converted into luxury villas with modern amenities and breathtaking views of the island.

No matter which villa or apartment you choose, be sure to book in advance to ensure availability and get the best rates. With so many great options to choose from, a villa or apartment is a great way to make your trip to the Greek Islands truly unforgettable.

Hostels and Guesthouses

Hostels and guesthouses are great options for travelers who are looking to save money, meet new people, and have a unique and authentic experience. These types of accommodations are often more intimate than hotels and allow you to connect with locals and other travelers in a way that you might not be able to in a larger, more impersonal setting.

One of the main differences between hostels and guesthouses is that hostels typically offer dormitory-style rooms with shared bathrooms, while guest houses usually offer private rooms with en suite bathrooms. Both options can be quite affordable, but if you're traveling with a group or looking for more privacy, a guesthouse might be the better choice.

When it comes to amenities, hostels and guesthouses vary widely. Some offer basic facilities like a communal kitchen and free Wi-Fi, while others have more luxurious features like swimming pools and on-site restaurants. It's important to do your research and read reviews to find a hostel or guesthouse that meets your specific needs and preferences.

One example of a popular hostel in the Greek Islands is the Youth Hostel Anna in Paros. This hostel offers dormitory-style rooms as well as private rooms, and has a beautiful outdoor terrace with stunning views of the sea. Another option is the Galini Pension in Naxos, which is a family-run guesthouse that offers comfortable rooms and a friendly atmosphere.

No matter which hostel or guesthouse you choose, it's important to remember that these types of accommodations are all about the experience. They offer a unique opportunity to connect with other travelers and to immerse yourself in the local culture.

Camping

Camping is a popular and unique way to experience the Greek Islands. It allows visitors to immerse themselves in nature and experience the beauty of the islands firsthand. There are many camping options available throughout the islands, ranging from basic tents to luxurious glamping options.

When it comes to camping in the Greek Islands, visitors have the option of staying at both organized and wild campsites. Organized campsites are equipped with basic amenities such as showers, toilets, and cooking facilities, while wild campsites are more primitive and require visitors to bring their own supplies. It's important to note that wild camping is not always legal in Greece, so it's important to check local laws and regulations before pitching a tent.

One of the most popular camping options in the Greek Islands is glamping. Glamping combines the experience of camping with the luxury of a hotel. Visitors can enjoy comfortable beds, electricity, and even air conditioning in some cases, all while being surrounded by the natural beauty of the islands. Some popular glamping options in the Greek Islands include Castello Camping in Naxos, Glamping Serifos in Serifos, and Koukounaries Camping in Skiathos.

For visitors looking for a more traditional camping experience, there are many options available as well. Camping Apollon in Paros offers basic tent camping with amenities such as a restaurant, a mini-market, and a swimming pool. Camping Thines in Kefalonia offers stunning views of the Ionian Sea and is equipped with a restaurant, a bar, and even a mini-golf course.

Camping is a unique and exciting way to experience the Greek Islands. Whether visitors choose to stay at a basic tent campsite or a luxurious glamping option, they are sure to be surrounded by the natural beauty and stunning scenery that the islands have to offer.

Chapter 5

The Islands

The Greek Islands are a collection of more than 6,000 islands and islets scattered throughout the Aegean and Ionian Seas. Known for their stunning landscapes, rich history, and vibrant culture, the Greek Islands have long been a favorite destination for travelers from all over the world. From the cosmopolitan atmosphere of Mykonos to the laid-back charm of Crete, each island offers a unique experience and a chance to explore some of the most beautiful and unspoiled corners of the Mediterranean.

In this chapter, we will take a closer look at the Greek Islands, their history, culture, and attractions, and provide a guide to help you plan your perfect island-hopping adventure. So grab your sunscreen, your camera, and your sense of adventure, and let's set sail for the magical world of the Greek Islands!

Cyclades Islands

The Cyclades Islands, located in the Aegean Sea, is a group of 220 islands known for its picturesque landscapes, ancient ruins, and vibrant culture. This archipelago is one of the most visited regions in Greece, attracting millions of tourists every year. If you're planning a trip to the Greek Islands, you definitely don't want to miss the Cyclades.

Santorini is perhaps the most famous island in the Cyclades, renowned for its stunning sunsets and picturesque whitewashed buildings. The island is also home to several must-see attractions, including the Akrotiri archaeological site, the Red Beach, and the towns of Fira and Oia. Fira offers a bustling nightlife, while Oia is known for its charming shops and stunning views of the Aegean Sea.

Mykonos is another popular Cyclades island, famous for its lively atmosphere, beautiful beaches, and charming windmills. The island is a favorite destination for party-goers, but it also offers plenty of cultural attractions, such as the Mykonos Archaeological Museum and the iconic Paraportiani Church.

Naxos, the largest island in the Cyclades, offers a more laid-back atmosphere compared to Mykonos and Santorini. It boasts some of the best beaches in the region, including Agios Prokopios and Agia Anna. Visitors can also explore the Portara, a massive ancient temple dedicated to Apollo, and the picturesque village of Apiranthos, which offers a glimpse into traditional Cycladic architecture.

Paros is another Cyclades island worth visiting, known for its villages, beautiful beaches, and excellent seafood. The island is also home to several historical sites, such as the Panagia Ekatontapiliani, a 6th-century Byzantine church, and the ancient marble quarries.

Other notable Cyclades islands include Ios, known for its party scene and stunning beaches, and Milos, which boasts unique geological formations and picturesque fishing villages.

When visiting the Cyclades, visitors should also take the time to experience the local culture and cuisine. Sample traditional dishes such as moussaka, souvlaki, and fava, and try local wines such as Assyrtiko and Vinsanto. The region is also famous for its vibrant festivals and celebrations, such as the Apokries Carnival and the Easter traditions of Corfu.

Overall, the Cyclades Islands offer a wealth of attractions and experiences that cater to a range of interests. From stunning beaches and ancient ruins to lively nightlife and delicious cuisine, there's something for everyone in this picturesque archipelago.

Ionian Islands

The Ionian Islands are a beautiful and captivating destination for any traveler looking to explore the Greek Islands. These islands are located in the western part of Greece. Here, we will take a closer look at the Ionian Islands, highlighting some of the top tourist attractions and things to do and see.

One of the most popular Ionian Islands is Corfu. This island is known for its Venetian-style architecture, beautiful beaches, and rich history. Visitors to Corfu can explore the UNESCO-listed Old Town, which is home to ancient fortresses, narrow streets, and beautiful mansions. Other top attractions on the island include the Achilleion Palace, the Mon Repos Estate, and the Corfu Museum of Asian Art. Beach lovers will enjoy spending time at the beaches of Paleokastritsa, Glyfada, and Agios Georgios.

Another must-visit Ionian Island is Zakynthos, also known as Zante. This island is famous for its stunning beaches, including the Shipwreck Beach, which is one of the most photographed beaches in the world. Visitors can also explore the Blue Caves, a series of sea caves with crystal-clear blue waters. For a unique experience, visitors can take a boat tour to see the endangered loggerhead sea turtles that nest on the island's beaches.

Kefalonia is another beautiful Ionian Island that is worth exploring. This island is known for its rugged coastline, stunning beaches, and breathtaking scenery. Visitors can take a stroll through the picturesque villages of Assos and Fiscardo, or explore the Melissani Cave, an underground lake with clear waters. Beach lovers can spend time at the famous Myrtos Beach, which is another beautiful beach in Greece.

The Ionian Islands also offer plenty of opportunities for outdoor activities. Visitors can go hiking or mountain biking in the lush green hills, or take a sailing or kayaking trip to explore the hidden coves and beaches. Foodies will enjoy trying out the local cuisine, which includes fresh seafood, grilled meats, and delicious pastries.

Overall, the Ionian Islands offer a unique and unforgettable travel experience for anyone looking to explore the Greek Islands. With their stunning scenery, rich history, and vibrant culture, these islands are sure to captivate and fascinate any visitor.

Dodecanese Islands

The Dodecanese Islands are a group of 15 large and 150 small islands located in the southeastern Aegean Sea. Each island in the Dodecanese has its own unique history, culture, and traditions, and boasts stunning natural beauty, clear waters, sandy beaches, picturesque villages, and ancient archaeological sites.

One of the most notable features of the Dodecanese Islands is their rich history, with several remarkable historical sites that are well-known around the world. The largest and most famous island in the Dodecanese is Rhodes, which is home to the Medieval Old Town of Rhodes, designated as a UNESCO World Heritage Site. The Old Town features a maze of narrow streets and alleys lined with ancient buildings, churches, and squares. The Palace of the Grand Master of the Knights of Rhodes is a must-see attraction for history enthusiasts.

Kos is another popular destination in the Dodecanese, with a rich history that dates back to the 4th century BC. One of the most significant archaeological sites on the island is the Asklepion, an ancient medical center. Visitors can also explore the ruins of the castle of the Knights of Saint John, a testament to the island's turbulent past.

Patmos, known as the "Island of the Apocalypse," is where Saint John wrote the Book of Revelation. The Monastery of Saint John and the Cave of the Apocalypse are both UNESCO World Heritage Sites and are considered the most significant religious sites in the Dodecanese.

Other notable islands in the Dodecanese include Symi, Leros, Kalymnos, and Karpathos. Symi is a charming island with colorful neoclassical architecture and stunning beaches, while Leros is known for its rugged landscape and picturesque fishing villages. Kalymnos is a mecca for rock climbers, with towering cliffs and challenging routes, and Karpathos is a haven for windsurfers, with strong winds and crystal clear waters.

In addition to their historical and cultural significance, the Dodecanese Islands offer a wide range of activities and attractions for visitors. Water sports such as snorkeling, diving, and sailing are popular, and many of the islands have excellent beaches for swimming and sunbathing. The islands also offer excellent hiking trails, with stunning vistas and picturesque villages along the way.

The food in the Dodecanese is another highlight, with traditional dishes that are both simple and delicious. Seafood is a staple, and visitors can enjoy fresh fish and seafood dishes at local tavernas. Local specialties include koulouri (a sesame-covered bread ring), souvlaki (grilled meat skewers), and dolmades (stuffed grape leaves).

The Dodecanese Islands are a fascinating destination for travelers who want to experience the rich culture, history, and natural beauty of Greece. With its unique mix of historical sites, stunning beaches, and traditional cuisine, the Dodecanese Islands offer something for everyone. Whether you're interested in history, adventure, or relaxation, the Dodecanese Islands are the perfect place to explore.

Saronic Islands

The Saronic Islands, situated in the Saronic Gulf of the Aegean Sea, are a group of small islands and islets with stunning beauty, rich history, and unique culture. Comprising seven main islands, each with its charm and character, the Saronic Islands are a must-visit destination for anyone planning a trip to Greece.

The islands are easily accessible from Athens, making them a popular destination for day trips and weekend getaways. Here's a comprehensive guide to help you plan your trip to the Saronic Islands.

Hydra

Hydra Island is a popular tourist spot in the Saronic Islands due to its picturesque architecture, clear waters, and untouched natural scenery. No cars or motorbikes are allowed on the island, making it perfect for those who want a tranquil and peaceful vacation.

Travelers can take pleasure in walking around the island's narrow streets, taking in the charming stone houses, and relaxing on the various beaches. The island's primary town, Hydra Town, houses several museums such as the Historical Archive Museum and the Ecclesiastical Museum.

Poros

Poros is another popular island in the Saronic Gulf, known for its picturesque town, stunning beaches, and historic landmarks. Visitors can explore the island's main town, which is situated on a narrow strip of land connecting two hills, and marvel at the neoclassical buildings and narrow alleys.

One of the main attractions of Poros is the Clock Tower, which offers stunning views of the town and the sea. The island is also home to several beaches, including Love Bay and Russian Bay, which are ideal for swimming and sunbathing.

Aegina

Aegina, the largest of the Saronic Islands, is a popular tourist destination known for its fascinating history, breathtaking beaches, and lively nightlife. Visitors can discover the island's ancient ruins, such as the Temple of Aphaia, and learn about its significant contribution to ancient Greek history.

The island boasts several beaches, including Agia Marina Beach and Marathonas Beach, which are perfect for swimming and a variety of water sports. Additionally, tourists can indulge in the vibrant nightlife of Aegina, with a plethora of bars, clubs, and restaurants situated in the primary town.

Spetses

Spetses is a small island situated just off the coast of the Peloponnese, known for its stunning beaches, charming town, and historic landmarks. Visitors can explore the island's main town, which is home to several neoclassical buildings and museums, including the Bouboulina Museum, dedicated to the Greek heroine Laskarina Bouboulina.

The island is also home to several beaches, including Agia Paraskevi Beach and Kaiki Beach, which are ideal for swimming and water sports. Visitors can also explore the island's natural beauty by hiking along the island's numerous trails, including the popular Old Coastal Path.

Agistri

Agistri, a charming island situated just a short ferry ride away from Athens, is renowned for its breathtaking beaches, crystal-clear waters, and untouched natural splendor. The island boasts several picturesque beaches, such as Aponissos Beach and Skala Beach, perfect for swimming and soaking up the sun's rays.

Furthermore, the island has a multitude of hiking trails to explore, with the Megalochori Trail being a popular choice. It provides visitors with awe-inspiring views of the island's natural beauty. The island's main town is also a must-visit destination, with its numerous restaurants and cafes serving traditional Greek cuisine.

The Saronic Islands are an absolute treasure of the Aegean Sea, offering visitors a unique combination of natural beauty, rich history, and distinct culture. Whether you prefer to unwind on the beach, discover ancient ruins, or immerse yourself in the local culture, the Saronic Islands have something for everyone.In addition to the five main islands mentioned above, the Saronic Gulf is also home to two smaller islands, namely Agios Georgios and Dokos.

Agios Georgios is a tiny island with no permanent residents, known for its stunning beach and crystal-clear waters, while Dokos is a small uninhabited island, ideal for those seeking a peaceful and secluded vacation.

Visitors to the Saronic Islands can explore the islands by ferry, with regular services connecting the islands to Athens and other nearby destinations. The islands are also home to several marinas, making them an ideal destination for those traveling by boat.

In terms of accommodation, the islands offer a wide range of options, from luxury resorts and boutique hotels to budget-friendly guesthouses and apartments. Visitors can also choose to stay in traditional stone houses or villas, offering an authentic Greek island experience.

When it comes to dining, the Saronic Islands are known for their delicious cuisine, with numerous restaurants and tavernas serving fresh seafood, local meats, and traditional Greek dishes. Visitors can also enjoy a variety of local wines and spirits, including the famous Greek ouzo.

The Saronic Islands are a unique and captivating destination, offering visitors a wide range of activities, attractions, and experiences. Whether you're looking to relax on the beach, explore ancient ruins, or immerse yourself in the local culture, the Saronic Islands are sure to leave you captivated and inspired. Plan your trip today and discover the beauty of this hidden gem in the Aegean Sea.

Euboea Island

Euboea Island, also known as Evia, is one of the largest islands in Greece, located just off the eastern coast of the mainland. With its rugged mountains, lush forests, crystal clear waters, and charming villages, it is a must-visit destination for any traveler looking to experience the best of Greek island life.

One of the island's top attractions is its stunning beaches. Euboea boasts a coastline of over 600 kilometers, with a variety of beaches to suit all tastes. Some of the most popular include Marmari Beach, with its soft white sands and turquoise waters, and Pefki Beach, which is surrounded by pine trees and offers excellent snorkeling opportunities. Other notable beaches include Kalamos, Lefkandi, and Vassiliki, all of which offer breathtaking views and a relaxing atmosphere.

In addition to its beaches, Euboea is also home to a number of fascinating historic sites. The island has a rich cultural heritage, with a history that dates back thousands of years. Some of the most notable sites include the ancient city of Eretria, which was once a major trading center in the ancient world, and the Byzantine Monastery of Saint David, which is located in the town of Prokopi and is considered one of the most important religious sites on the island.

For nature lovers, Euboea has plenty to offer as well. The island is home to a number of stunning natural attractions, including the Dimosari Gorge, which is known for its stunning waterfalls and crystal clear pools, and the Ochi Mountain Range, which offers spectacular views of the surrounding landscape. Visitors can also explore the island's numerous hiking trails, which offer the perfect opportunity to get up close and personal with the island's diverse flora and fauna.

In terms of cuisine, Euboea is known for its fresh seafood, which is caught daily by local fishermen. Visitors can sample a variety of delicious dishes, such as grilled octopus, fried calamari, and traditional fish souvlaki. The island is also known for its excellent wine, with a number of local vineyards producing high-quality varieties.

For those looking for a more active holiday, Euboea has plenty of activities to keep visitors entertained. Water sports such as windsurfing and kitesurfing are popular in many of the island's coastal towns, while horse riding and mountain biking are also popular activities for those who prefer to stay on land. Visitors can also explore the island's many charming villages, each with unique character and traditional architecture.

In addition to its natural and cultural attractions, Euboea Island is also home to charming towns and villages. The island's capital, Chalkida, is a bustling port town with a rich history dating back to ancient times. Visitors can explore the town's many historic sites, including the ancient walls and gates, the Roman Aqueduct, and the Byzantine Castle.

Another must-visit town is Eretria, which was once a major center of trade and culture in the ancient world. Visitors can explore the town's many archaeological sites, including the ancient theater and the Temple of Apollo Daphnephoros. Eretria is also home to a number of excellent museums, including the Archaeological Museum, which features a collection of artifacts dating back to the Neolithic era.

For those looking for a more laid-back atmosphere, the town of Edipsos is a popular destination. Located on the northern coast of the island, Edipsos is popular for its natural hot springs, which are said to have healing properties. Visitors can soak in the springs and enjoy the town's relaxed atmosphere, which is perfect for those looking to unwind and recharge.

Euboea Island is also home to a number of cultural festivals and events throughout the year. One of the most popular is the Carnival of Kimi, which takes place in the town of Kimi in February. The festival features colorful parades, traditional music and dance, and plenty of delicious food and drink. Other notable festivals include the Grape Harvest Festival in September and the Feast of Saint David in November.

Whether you desire a relaxing beach holiday, an adventure-filled outdoor experience, or a cultural immersion in ancient Greek history, Euboea Island has something for everyone. With its stunning natural beauty, rich cultural heritage, and friendly local communities, it is a destination that should not be missed by any traveler to Greece.

Tips for Travelers

If you're planning a trip to the Sporades Islands, here are some tips to help you make the most of your visit:

Book accommodation in advance: The Sporades Islands are popular with tourists, especially during the high season. It's important to book your accommodation in advance to avoid disappointment.

Pack for the weather: The weather in the Sporades Islands can be unpredictable, so it's important to pack for all eventualities. Bring lightweight clothes for the warm days and a jacket or sweater for the cooler evenings.

Rent a car or scooter: To fully explore the islands, it's a good idea to rent a car or scooter. This will give you the flexibility to visit all the tourist attractions and beautiful beaches at your own pace.

Try the local cuisine: The Sporades Islands are famous for their delicious seafood and local delicacies. Be sure to try the local cuisine at the traditional tavernas and restaurants.

Respect the environment: The Sporades Islands are home to a unique and fragile ecosystem. It's important to respect the environment and avoid littering or damaging the natural habitats.

The Sporades Islands are a hidden gem of the Aegean Sea, offering visitors a unique and unforgettable holiday experience. With their stunning natural beauty, clear waters, and rich history and culture, the islands are a must-visit destination for any traveler. From exploring ancient ruins and traditional villages to relaxing on the beautiful beaches and trying the delicious local cuisine, there's something for everyone in the Sporades Islands. Follow these tips to make the most of your visit and create memories that will last a lifetime.

The Sporades Islands

The Sporades Islands are located off the eastern coast of Greece and consist of 24 islands, of which only four are permanently inhabited: Skopelos, Skiathos, Alonissos, and Skyros. These islands are known for their crystal-clear waters, charming towns, and beautiful beaches. They are a popular destination for tourists seeking a unique Greek island experience. In this chapter, we will take an in-depth look at the Sporades Islands and highlight some of the must-visit attractions, things to do, and places to see.

Skiathos

Skiathos is the most popular and vibrant of the Sporades Islands, offering a lively atmosphere, a bustling nightlife, and some beautiful beaches in Greece. Koukounaries Beach is a famous beach on the island, known for its stunning turquoise waters, golden sand, and pine trees. Other popular beaches include Lalaria Beach, Banana Beach, and Agia Paraskevi Beach. Skiathos Town, the island's capital, is a charming blend of traditional architecture, narrow streets, and modern amenities. The town is home to a plethora of restaurants, cafes, and bars, making it the perfect place to unwind after a day at the beach.

Skopelos

Skopelos is a peaceful and serene island, known for its natural beauty, picturesque villages, and traditional way of life. The island's most famous attraction is the stunning chapel of Agios Ioannis Kastri, which sits atop a rocky outcrop overlooking the Aegean Sea. This chapel gained international fame after it was featured in the movie "Mamma Mia!".

Skopelos Town is a charming port town with a maze of narrow streets, whitewashed houses, and traditional tavernas. Other notable attractions on the island include the medieval castle of Skopelos, the traditional village of Glossa, and the beautiful beaches of Stafylos, Panormos, and Kastani.

Alonissos

Alonissos is the most remote and untouched of the Sporades Islands, offering visitors a chance to experience the unspoiled beauty of the Aegean Sea. The island is home to the National Marine Park of Alonissos, which was established to protect the endangered Mediterranean monk seal. Visitors can take a boat tour of the park and observe the seals in their natural habitat.

The island's capital, Patitiri, is a charming village with a picturesque harbor, traditional tavernas, and a lively nightlife scene. Other popular attractions on the island include the traditional villages of Chora and Steni Vala, the beautiful beaches of Chrisi Milia, and Leftos Gialos.

Skyros

Skyros is the southernmost of the Sporades Islands, offering visitors a unique blend of natural beauty, rich history, and traditional culture. The island's most famous attraction is the Byzantine Monastery of Saint George, which sits atop a hill overlooking the town of Skyros. The monastery is home to a collection of ancient manuscripts and icons, making it a must-visit destination for history buffs.

Skyros Town is a charming and traditional village, known for its narrow streets, white houses, and blue-domed churches. Other notable attractions on the island include the beautiful beaches of Magazia, Molos, and Atsitsa, and the traditional village of Pouria.

The Sporades Islands are a hidden gem in the Aegean Sea, offering visitors a unique Greek island experience. Each island has its own distinct charm, from the vibrant atmosphere of Skiathos to the untouched natural beauty of Alonissos. Visitors can enjoy a range of activities, from swimming in crystal-clear waters to exploring traditional

North Aegean Islands

The North Aegean Islands are a group of islands located in the northeastern part of the Aegean Sea. This group consists of nine main islands: Samos, Lesvos, Ikaria, Chios, Lemnos, Thassos, Agios Efstratios, Psara, and Inousses. Each island has its charm, with a rich history, picturesque villages, and beautiful beaches. Let us take a closer look at the North Aegean Islands and highlight some of the must-visit attractions, things to do, and places to see.

Lesvos

Lesvos is the third-largest Greek. The island is famous for its olive groves and the production of ouzo, a traditional Greek alcoholic drink. Visitors can explore the island's capital, Mytilene, which is home to a Venetian castle, a lively market, and a range of restaurants and cafes. The island is also home to the Petrified Forest, a UNESCO World Heritage site, which features fossilized tree trunks that date back millions of years. Other popular attractions include the traditional villages of Molyvos and Agiassos and the beautiful beaches of Vatera, Eresos, and Skala Kallonis.

Chios

Chios is a large island known for its medieval villages, Byzantine monasteries, and beautiful beaches. The island is famous for its production of mastic, a resin that is used in medicine, cosmetics, and cooking. Visitors can explore the island's capital, Chios Town, which is home to a medieval castle, a range of museums, and a bustling market. The island is also home to the Nea Moni Monastery, a UNESCO World Heritage site that dates back to the 11th century. Other popular attractions include the traditional villages of Pyrgi and Mesta and the beautiful beaches of Mavra Volia, Karfas, and Elinda.

Samos

Samos is a green and mountainous island popular for its natural beauty, ancient ruins, and beautiful beaches. The island is famous for its production of sweet wine, which has been popular since ancient times. Visitors can explore the island's capital, Vathy, which is a charming port town with a range of restaurants, cafes, and bars. The island is also home to the Heraion of Samos, a UNESCO World Heritage site that was dedicated to the goddess Hera. Other popular attractions are the ancient ruins of the Temple of Pythagoras, the traditional village of Kokkari, and the beautiful beaches of Potokaki, Tsamadou, and Lemonakia.

Ikaria

Ikaria is a small and mountainous island known for its natural hot springs, traditional villages, and laid-back way of life. The island is famous for its longevity, with a high percentage of residents living well into their 90s and beyond. Visitors can explore the island's capital, Agios Kirykos, which is a charming town with a range of traditional tavernas and cafes.

The island is also home to the Therma Hot Springs, which are said to have therapeutic properties. Other popular attractions include the traditional village of Armenistis, the ruins of the ancient city of Nas, and the beautiful beaches of Seychelles, Livadi, and Messakti.

Lemnos

Lemnos is a small and unspoiled island known for its natural beauty, traditional way of life, and stunning beaches. The island is famous for its production of wine, cheese, and honey, which are all made using traditional methods. Visitors can explore the island's capital, Myrina, which is a charming port town with a range of restaurants, cafes, and bars.

The town is home to a Venetian castle that offers panoramic views of the island. The island is also home to the ancient ruins of Hephaestia, which was once the capital of the island. Other popular attractions include the traditional villages of Moudros and Plati, and the beautiful beaches of Keros, Fanaraki, and Thanos.

Thassos

Thassos is a green and mountainous island known for its pristine beaches, charming villages, and rich history. The island is famous for its production of marble, which has been used to create many famous works of art throughout history. Visitors can explore the island's capital, Limenas, which is a charming port town with a range of restaurants, cafes, and shops.

The town is home to the ancient ruins of the Acropolis and the Ancient Agora. Other popular attractions include the traditional villages of Panagia and Theologos, and the beautiful beaches of Golden Beach, Marble Beach, and Paradise Beach.

Agios Efstratios

Agios Efstratios, a small and secluded island nestled between the beautiful Greek islands of Lesvos and Limnos, offers a unique and unforgettable experience for visitors. This hidden gem boasts breathtaking natural beauty, with crystal-clear waters and a diverse array of flora and fauna that make it a must-visit destination for nature lovers.

The island's capital, Agios Efstratios Town, is a charming and picturesque village that offers a glimpse into the island's rich history and culture. With its traditional white-washed houses and narrow streets, visitors can immerse themselves in the island's unique architecture and enjoy a peaceful stroll through the quaint and tranquil streets.

One of the island's main attractions is the Agios Efstratios National Park, a protected area that is home to a diverse range of bird species and unique plant life. Nature enthusiasts will love exploring the park's many trails and witnessing the stunning beauty of the island's wildlife and landscapes.

Psara

Psara is a small and remote island located between Chios and Lesvos. The island is known for its rugged terrain, traditional way of life, and beautiful beaches. Visitors can explore the island's capital, Psara Town, which is a charming village with a range of traditional tavernas and cafes. The town is home to a number of monuments and museums that highlight the island's rich history. The island is also home to the Agios Nikolaos Monastery, which is a beautiful example of traditional Greek architecture. Other popular attractions include the beautiful beaches of Fasolou and Tsigouri.

Inousses

Inousses, a petite and secluded island nestled near Chios, boasts of natural beauty that can leave any visitor awestruck. The pristine and crystal-clear waters, combined with the traditional way of life, make it an ideal destination for travelers seeking a tranquil getaway. Inousses Town, the island's capital, is a delightful village characterized by its white-washed houses and winding streets that add to its charm.

Explorers can immerse themselves in the island's rich history by visiting the town's museums and monuments. The Monastery of Panagia, with its exquisite traditional Greek architecture, is an excellent example of the island's cultural heritage. Visitors can also indulge in the serene and stunning beaches of Fyonisi and Port Leone, which are popular tourist spots.

The North Aegean Islands, a picturesque and diverse group of islands, cater to every traveler's tastes. From the stunning natural beauty of Lesvos and Samos to the rugged terrain of Psara and the isolated charm of Agios Efstratios and Inousses, each island has a unique and distinctive character. Tourists can delve into the past by exploring ancient ruins, visit quaint and traditional villages, or spend a day basking in the sun on one of the gorgeous beaches.

The region is also famous for its delicious local cuisine and wine, which will tantalize the taste buds of any foodie. The North Aegean Islands is a perfect destination, whether one is looking for a relaxing beach holiday or an adventure-filled trip.

Northern Sporades Islands

The Northern Sporades Islands are a group of picturesque islands in Greece that offer an unforgettable travel experience for visitors. Situated in the Aegean Sea, this archipelago comprises 11 islands, of which only four are inhabited. This region is well-known for its lush greenery, crystal clear waters, and stunning beaches that are considered among the best in Greece. In this chapter, we'll take a closer look at the Northern Sporades Islands and discover what makes them so unique and fascinating.

Skiathos Island is the most popular island in the Northern Sporades, boasting a lively atmosphere and a range of tourist attractions. With over 60 beaches, visitors are spoilt for choice when it comes to sunbathing and swimming. Koukounaries Beach, Lalaria Beach, and Banana Beach are some of the most popular beaches on the island. Other attractions on Skiathos include the Bourtzi Fortress, the Old Port, and the Monastery of Evangelistria.

Skopelos Island is another popular destination in the Northern Sporades, famous for its stunning landscapes and charming villages. The island's capital, Skopelos Town, is a picturesque village with traditional houses, narrow streets, and a beautiful harbor. The Stafylos Beach, Kastani Beach, and Panormos Beach are some of the most popular beaches on the island. Visitors can also visit the Mamma Mia Church, where the famous movie was filmed.

Alonissos Island is a secluded island in the Northern Sporades, known for its unspoiled nature and crystal clear waters. The island is home to the National Marine Park of Alonissos, a protected area that hosts a range of marine life, including dolphins and monk seals. Visitors can explore the park by boat or take a hiking trail through the island's rugged terrain. Other attractions on Alonissos include the Chora, a traditional village with stunning views of the sea, and the Agios Dimitrios Beach.

Skyros Island is the largest island in the Northern Sporades, offering a unique blend of history, culture, and natural beauty. The island is home to the Skyros Horse, a rare breed that is found only on the island. Visitors can take a horseback ride through the island's lush forests and rugged terrain. Other attractions on Skyros include the Skyros Castle, the Manos Faltaits Museum, and the Molos Beach.

When visiting the Northern Sporades Islands, there are plenty of activities to keep visitors entertained. Water sports such as snorkeling, diving, and windsurfing are popular among tourists, and there are plenty of rental shops and tour operators that offer these activities. Hiking and cycling are also great ways to explore the islands' rugged terrain and stunning landscapes. Visitors can rent a bike or join a guided hiking tour to explore the islands' hidden gems.

Accommodation options in the Northern Sporades Islands range from luxury resorts to budget-friendly guesthouses and apartments. Visitors can choose to stay in a traditional village or a modern resort, depending on their preference. Skiathos, Skopelos, and Alonissos have various accommodation options, including hotels, villas, and apartments. Skyros has fewer options, but visitors can still find comfortable and affordable accommodation in the island's villages.

When it comes to dining, the Northern Sporades Islands offer a wide range of culinary delights. Seafood is a specialty on these islands, and visitors can sample fresh fish, octopus, and squid at local tavernas and restaurants.

Traditional Greek dishes such as laki, moussaka, souvand Greek salad are also widely available. Visitors can also indulge in local delicacies such as Skopelos cheese pie and almond sweets.

The Northern Sporades Islands are well-connected by ferry and boat services. Visitors can reach the islands from the mainland port of Volos, which is located about 20 km from the islands. There are also ferry services that connect the islands to other popular destinations in Greece, such as Athens, Thessaloniki, and Crete. Visitors can also explore the islands by boat, either by renting a private boat or joining a guided tour.

In terms of weather, the Northern Sporades Islands enjoy a Mediterranean climate, with mild winters and hot summers. The best time to visit is between May and September, when the weather is warm and sunny, and the sea is calm and inviting. July and August are the peak tourist season, and the islands can get crowded during this time. Visitors who prefer a quieter experience should consider visiting in May, June, or September.

The Northern Sporades Islands are a hidden gem in Greece, offering a unique travel experience that is sure to enchant and inspire visitors. From stunning beaches and charming villages to unspoiled nature and a rich culinary tradition, these islands have something for everyone. Whether you're looking for adventure, relaxation, or cultural immersion, the Northern Sporades Islands are the perfect destination for your next trip to Greece.

Argo-Saronic Islands

The Argo-Saronic Islands are a group of islands located in the Saronic Gulf, just off the coast of mainland Greece. These islands are known for their picturesque landscapes, crystal-clear waters, and rich history. In this chapter, we will explore everything you need to know about the Argo-Saronic Islands, including tourist attractions, things to do and see, and how to make the most out of your trip.

Aegina

The island of Aegina is one of the most popular destinations in the Argo-Saronic Islands. It is located just a short ferry ride away from Athens, making it a perfect day trip destination. Aegina is known for its beautiful beaches, stunning landscapes, and ancient history. The Temple of Aphaia, located on a hill overlooking the sea, is one of the most famous ancient sites on the island. The temple was built in the 5th century BC and is considered one of the best-preserved ancient temples in Greece. Visitors can also explore the picturesque town of Aegina, with its traditional architecture and colorful buildings. Don't forget to try the famous pistachios that are grown on the island!

Hydra

Hydra is a small, charming island located in the Saronic Gulf. The island is known for its beautiful architecture, picturesque harbor, and stunning views. There are no cars on the island, so visitors can explore the island on foot or by donkey. The town of Hydra is full of narrow streets, white-washed buildings, and traditional tavernas. One of the most popular attractions on the island is the Hydra Museum Historical Archives, which showcases the island's rich history and culture. Visitors can also enjoy swimming at one of the island's many beaches, or take a boat trip to explore the nearby islands and secluded coves.

Poros

Poros is a small, idyllic island located just a short ferry ride from Athens. The island is famous for its stunning beaches and picturesque landscapes. Visitors can explore the charming town of Poros, with its traditional architecture and colorful buildings. One of the most popular attractions on the island is the Clock Tower, which offers stunning views of the island and the surrounding sea. Visitors can also take a boat trip to explore the nearby beaches and coves, or go hiking in the island's beautiful countryside.

Spetses

Spetses is a small, picturesque island located in the Saronic Gulf. The island is popular for its beautiful beaches, clear waters, and stunning landscapes. Visitors can explore the charming town of Spetses, with its traditional architecture and colorful buildings. One of the most popular attractions on the island is the Bouboulina Museum, which is dedicated to the life and achievements of the famous Greek heroine Laskarina Bouboulina. Visitors can also enjoy swimming at one of the island's many beaches, or take a boat trip to explore the nearby islands and secluded coves.

The Argo-Saronic Islands are easily accessible from Athens. Visitors can take a ferry from Piraeus port, which is located just a short distance from the city center. The ferry ride takes around one hour, depending on the destination, and offers stunning views of the Saronic Gulf.

Alternatively, visitors can take a hydrofoil or catamaran, which are faster but more expensive. There are also several private boat operators that offer tours of the islands, which is a great way to see multiple islands in one day.

The best time to visit the Argo-Saronic Islands is during the summer months, from June to September. During this time, the weather is warm and sunny, and the waters are perfect for swimming and water sports. However, it is also the busiest time of the year, so visitors should expect large crowds and higher prices.

If you prefer a quieter and more relaxed experience, consider visiting in the shoulder seasons, from April to June or September to November. During these times, the weather is still pleasant, and there are fewer tourists, making it easier to explore the islands at your own pace.

Each island in the Argo-Saronic Islands has its own unique charm and accommodations. Visitors can choose from a range of hotels, apartments, and villas, depending on their budget and preferences.

In Aegina, visitors can stay in the town center, where they will be close to the main attractions and amenities. Hydra has a range of boutique hotels and guesthouses, many of which offer stunning views of the harbor. Poros has several beachfront hotels and apartments, which are perfect for those who want to be close to the sea. Spetses has a range of luxury hotels and villas, which offer a more upscale experience.

The Argo-Saronic Islands are a group of islands that offer a unique and unforgettable experience for visitors. With their stunning landscapes, crystal-clear waters, and rich history, these islands are the perfect destination for those who want to explore the beauty and culture of Greece. From the ancient temples of Aegina to the charming town of Hydra, there is something for everyone in the Argo-Saronic Islands.

Chapter 6

Top Attractions

The Greek islands have been a popular tourist destination for decades, and for good reason. The stunning landscapes, crystal-clear waters, and rich history and culture of the islands draw visitors from around the world. From the vibrant nightlife of Mykonos to the ancient ruins of Rhodes, each island has its own unique charm and appeal.

In this chapter, we will explore the top attractions of the Greek islands, from the iconic landmarks to the hidden gems waiting to be discovered. Whether you are seeking relaxation, adventure, or a taste of Greek culture, there is something for everyone in these beautiful island paradises.

Ancient Ruins

The Greek Islands are home to some of the most remarkable ancient ruins in the world. From towering temples to sprawling amphitheaters, exploring the ancient ruins of the Greek Islands is a fascinating journey through history.

One of the most famous ancient ruins in Greece is the Acropolis in Athens, but there are many more ruins to discover on the Greek Islands. Visitors can explore the ancient city of Knossos on the island of Crete, which dates back to the Bronze Age. The ruins here include the impressive Palace of Knossos, which was once the center of Minoan civilization and a hub of political and economic activity.

The island of Delos is another must-see destination for history enthusiasts. This tiny island was once the center of the Cyclades and an important religious center in ancient Greece. Visitors can explore the ruins of the Temple of Apollo, the ancient theater, and the agora, which was once a bustling marketplace.

For those interested in ancient Greek architecture, the island of Rhodes is a must-visit destination. Here, visitors can explore the ancient city of Lindos, which features a well-preserved acropolis and towering temples dedicated to Athena and Zeus.

Another fascinating site is the ancient city of Samos, which is located on the island of the same name. Here, visitors can explore the remains of the Temple of Hera, which was once one of the largest temples in Greece, as well as the ancient theater and Roman baths.

On the island of Santorini, visitors can explore the ancient city of Akrotiri, which was buried by volcanic ash in the 17th century BC. The ruins here include well-preserved buildings, frescoes, and pottery that offer a glimpse into life in ancient Greece.

There are many other ancient ruins to explore on the Greek Islands, each with its own unique history and charm. Visitors can explore the ancient city of Eleusis on the Attica peninsula, the ruins of the ancient city of Corinth, or the ancient city of Mycenae, which was once home to the legendary King Agamemnon.

Exploring the ancient ruins of the Greek Islands is a fascinating journey through history. Visitors can marvel at the architectural prowess of ancient Greek builders, learn about the daily lives of ancient Greeks, and appreciate the cultural and historical significance of these remarkable ruins. Whether you're a history enthusiast or simply looking for a unique and captivating travel experience, the ancient ruins of the Greek Islands are not to be missed.

Beaches

The Greek Islands are a perfect destination for beach lovers. With over 200 inhabited islands and countless beaches, there's always a place to lay down your towel and soak up the Mediterranean sun. From secluded coves to lively resorts, Greek Island beaches offer something for everyone. In this chapter, we will explore the top beaches of the Greek Islands and what makes them unique.

Mykonos - Paradise Beach

Mykonos is a lively island known for its nightlife, but it also boasts some of the best beaches in Greece. One of the popular beaches on the island is Paradise Beach, which is famous for its clear waters, fine sand, and vibrant atmosphere. Visitors can rent sunbeds and umbrellas, grab a drink at one of the beach bars, or try their hand at watersports. At night, the beach transforms into a party destination, with live DJs and dancing.

Santorini - Red Beach

Santorini is known for its stunning caldera views, but the island's beaches are equally impressive. Red Beach, located near the village of Akrotiri, is one of the most unique beaches in Greece. The beach is named after the red volcanic rocks that surround it, creating a striking contrast with the deep blue waters of the Aegean Sea. Visitors can access the beach via a short hike from the parking lot or by boat.

Crete - Elafonisi Beach

Crete is the largest island in Greece and offers a wide variety of beaches. Elafonisi Beach, located on the southwestern coast of the island, is a must-visit for its pink sand and shallow turquoise waters. The beach is situated on a small island connected to the mainland by a sandbank, creating a lagoon-like setting. Visitors can rent sunbeds and umbrellas, grab a snack at the beach bar, or explore the nearby nature reserve.

Rhodes - Lindos Beach

Rhodes is a popular tourist destination with a long history and stunning beaches. Lindos Beach, located in the picturesque village of Lindos, is one of the island's top beaches. The beach is surrounded by rocky cliffs and offers clear waters, soft sand, and plenty of sunbeds and umbrellas for rent. Visitors can also explore the nearby Acropolis of Lindos, an important archaeological site in Greece.

Corfu - Canal d'Amour Beach

Corfu is a green island with a rich cultural heritage and beautiful beaches. Canal d'Amour Beach, located on the northwestern coast of the island, is a unique beach formation that features impressive rock formations and small caves. Visitors can swim in the shallow waters or explore the caves by boat. The beach is also known for its romantic atmosphere, as legend has it that couples who swim together in the canal will stay together forever.

The Greek Islands offer a diverse range of beaches, each with its own unique features and attractions. Whether you're looking for a lively party beach or a secluded cove, there's a beach for everyone. From the pink sands of Elafonisi Beach to the red rocks of Red Beach, the Greek Island beaches are a true wonder of nature. So pack your sunscreen, grab your towel, and get ready to experience the best beaches in Greece.

Churches and Monasteries

The Greek islands are known for their rich history and culture, and one of the most fascinating aspects of this culture is the wealth of churches and monasteries that can be found throughout the islands. These religious structures offer visitors a glimpse into the spiritual life of Greece, and they are often some of the most beautiful and awe-inspiring attractions on the islands.

Churches and monasteries are an important part of Greek culture, and they are often located in stunning natural settings, offering visitors the chance to experience the beauty of the islands while also exploring the history and culture of the area. Whether you are interested in art, history, or religion, there is sure to be a church or monastery on the Greek islands that will captivate and fascinate you.

One of the top attractions on many of the Greek islands is the stunning array of churches and monasteries that can be found there. For example, on the island of Crete, visitors can explore the beautiful Arkadi Monastery, which dates back to the 16th century and played a key role in the island's fight for independence from the Ottoman Empire. The monastery's stunning architecture and rich history make it a must-visit for people visiting Crete.

On the island of Santorini, visitors can explore the famous Church of Panagia Episkopi, which dates back to the 11th century and is one of the oldest churches on the island. The church's beautiful frescoes and stunning architecture make it a popular destination for visitors from all over the world.

Other notable churches and monasteries on the Greek islands include the Monastery of St. John the Theologian on the island of Patmos, which is said to be the place where St. John wrote the Book of Revelation, and the Monastery of Hozoviotissa on the island of Amorgos, which is built into the side of a cliff and offers amazing views of the Aegean Sea.

In addition to their historical and religious significance, many of the churches and monasteries on the Greek islands offer visitors the chance to participate in religious ceremonies and festivals. These events can be a great way to experience the local culture and to connect with the local community.

When visiting churches and monasteries on the Greek islands, it is important to be respectful of the local customs and traditions. Visitors should dress modestly and avoid taking photographs inside the churches and monasteries unless they are given permission to do so.

Overall, the churches and monasteries of the Greek islands are a fascinating and beautiful aspect of the area's rich history and culture. They offer visitors the chance to explore the spiritual side of Greece while also experiencing the natural beauty of the islands. Whether you are a history buff, an art lover, or simply someone who appreciates the beauty of religious architecture, there is sure to be a church or monastery on the Greek islands that will captivate and inspire you.

Museums

As you embark on your journey to explore the beautiful Greek islands, one of the attractions that should not be missed is the museums. Greek museums are known for their rich collections of artifacts, sculptures, and other important historical treasures that tell the story of ancient Greece.

There are several museums spread across the Greek islands, each with a unique collection that reflects the rich cultural heritage of the Greek people. Here are some of the top museums to visit during your island hopping adventure:

The Acropolis Museum, Athens

Located at the foot of the Acropolis in Athens, this museum is a must-visit for history buffs. It houses a collection of ancient artifacts, including sculptures, pottery, and other objects that were found during excavations of the Acropolis site. The museum is designed to showcase the importance of the Acropolis in Greek history and culture.

Archaeological Museum of Delos, Delos Island

The island of Delos is known as the birthplace of Apollo, the god of music and light. The Archaeological Museum of Delos houses a collection of artifacts that tell the story of the island's ancient history. The museum is located in the center of the island, and visitors can see statues, pottery, and other objects that date back to the 7th century BC.

Museum of Prehistoric Thera, Santorini

Santorini is known for its stunning sunsets and beautiful beaches, but it also has a rich history that is worth exploring. The Museum of Prehistoric Thera in Santorini is located in Fira, the capital of the island. It showcases artifacts from the prehistoric era, including pottery, jewelry, and frescoes that were discovered during excavations of the Akrotiri site.

Museum of Naxos, Naxos Island

Naxos Island is the largest of the Cyclades islands and has a long history dating back to ancient times. The Museum of Naxos is located in the old town and houses a collection of artifacts that date back to the Mycenaean period. Visitors can see pottery, sculptures, and other objects that tell the story of the island's rich history.

Byzantine Museum, Chios Island

Chios Island is known for its medieval villages and stunning beaches, but it also has a rich Byzantine history. The Byzantine Museum in Chios is located in the castle of Chios and houses a collection of Byzantine artifacts, including icons, mosaics, and frescoes.

When visiting these museums, it's important to note that some may have entry fees, so be sure to check ahead of time. It's also a good idea to bring a guidebook or hire a guide to help you navigate the exhibits and understand the historical significance of the artifacts.

Visiting museums on the Greek islands is a great way to learn about the rich cultural heritage of Greece. From the Acropolis Museum in Athens to the Museum of Naxos on Naxos Island, each museum offers a unique collection of artifacts that tells the story of ancient Greece. Be sure to add these museums to your list of must-see attractions when exploring the Greek islands.

Chapter 7

Food and Drink

Food and drink are an integral part of any travel experience. Sampling local cuisine and beverages can provide insights into a region's culture, traditions, and way of life. From street food stalls to high-end restaurants, the food and drink scene is an exciting aspect of any journey.

Let us explore the delicious culinary delights and refreshing drinks that the Greek Islands have to offer. We will delve into the traditional dishes, fresh seafood, and local wines, as well as highlight the best places to dine and drink. Get ready to tantalize your taste buds and quench your thirst as we embark on a culinary journey through the Greek Islands.

Traditional Greek Cuisine

Greek cuisine is known for its flavorful and healthy dishes that are often made with fresh and locally-sourced ingredients. With its strong emphasis on vegetables, legumes, seafood, and olive oil, traditional Greek cuisine is a delight for both meat-eaters and vegetarians alike. In this chapter, we will explore the various traditional dishes that visitors can expect to encounter on their travels to the Greek islands.

Meze

One of the most famous elements of Greek cuisine is meze, which refers to small dishes that are often shared as appetizers or snacks. Popular meze dishes include tzatziki (yogurt and cucumber dip), dolmades (stuffed grape leaves), melitzanosalata (eggplant dip), fava (split pea dip), and keftedes (meatballs). Meze is typically enjoyed with a glass of ouzo, a traditional Greek spirit made from anise.

Seafood

As the Greek islands are surrounded by the Aegean Sea, seafood is a staple of the local cuisine. Visitors can expect to find fresh seafood dishes such as grilled octopus, fried calamari, and baked fish. One popular seafood dish that originated in Santorini is the lobster pasta, which features tender chunks of lobster meat in a rich tomato sauce.

Greek Salad

A Greek salad is a classic dish that can be found throughout Greece. This simple but delicious salad typically features fresh tomatoes, cucumbers, red onions, and feta cheese, dressed with olive oil and oregano. It is the perfect side dish to any meal or can be enjoyed on its own as a light lunch.

Moussaka

Moussaka is a hearty casserole dish that is a staple of Greek cuisine. It is made with layers of sliced eggplant, minced meat, and béchamel sauce, topped with a layer of cheese and baked until golden brown. This dish is a must-try for visitors to Greece and is often served as a main course.

Souvlaki

Souvlaki is a popular street food that consists of skewered meat (typically pork or chicken) that has been marinated in lemon juice, in olive oil, and herbs, and then grilled over an open flame. It is often served with a side of pita bread, tzatziki, and fresh tomatoes and onions.

Baklava

No discussion of Greek cuisine would be complete without mentioning baklava. This sweet pastry is made with layers of chopped nuts, phyllo dough, and honey syrup, and is often garnished with cinnamon and cloves. It is a delicious dessert that can be found at bakeries and cafes throughout Greece.

In addition to these traditional dishes, visitors to the Greek islands can also enjoy a variety of other delicacies such as spanakopita (spinach pie), pastitsio (a pasta and meat casserole), and avgolemono soup (a lemon and egg soup). It is also worth trying some of the local wines, such as the Assyrtiko and Santorini wines from Santorini or the Robola wine from Kefalonia.

Local Specialties

When it comes to experiencing the culinary delights of Greece, the Greek Islands are a treasure trove of gastronomic wonders waiting to be discovered. From fresh seafood to succulent lamb dishes and sweet treats, the local specialties of the Greek Islands are sure to tantalize your taste buds.

Let's start with the seafood. The Greek Islands are surrounded by crystal clear waters that are home to a variety of fish and seafood. One of the most popular dishes is grilled octopus, served with a drizzle of olive oil and a sprinkle of oregano. Another favorite is squid stuffed with feta cheese and fresh herbs, served with a side of lemon potatoes. Don't forget to try the traditional Greek fish soup, kakavia, made with a variety of fish and flavored with onions, garlic, and tomato.

If you're a meat lover, you won't be disappointed. One of the most famous dishes is lamb roasted on a spit, known as souvlaki. The meat is marinated in lemon juice, olive oil, and herbs and then grilled to perfection. Another popular dish is kleftiko, lamb or goat cooked in a sealed clay pot with vegetables and potatoes until tender and juicy.

Vegetarians will also find plenty of options. One of the most famous dishes is spanakopita, a savory pastry filled with spinach, feta cheese, and herbs. Another favorite is dolmades, vine leaves stuffed with rice and herbs. And don't forget to try the famous Greek salad, a refreshing mix of tomatoes, onions, cucumbers, and feta cheese, dressed with olive oil and lemon juice.

When it comes to sweet treats, the Greek Islands have plenty to offer. One of the most famous is loukoumades, small fried doughnuts drizzled with honey and cinnamon. Another favorite is baklava, layers of phyllo pastry filled with nuts and soaked in syrup. And for a truly unique experience, try the traditional Greek liqueur, ouzo, flavored with anise.

In terms of drinks, the Greek Islands are famous for their wine. Each island has its own unique varieties, so be sure to try a few. And don't forget to try the famous Greek coffee, served thick and strong in small cups.

Of course, no trip to the Greek Islands is complete without a visit to the local tavernas and restaurants. Here you can not only enjoy the delicious local specialties, but also soak up the lively atmosphere and traditional Greek hospitality.

In terms of tourist attractions and things to do, there is plenty to keep you busy. From exploring ancient ruins and museums to soaking up the sun on golden beaches and swimming in crystal clear waters. Don't miss the opportunity to visit the famous Acropolis in Athens, the stunning beaches of Santorini, or the historic town of Rhodes.

The local specialties of the Greek Islands are a true delight for the senses. From fresh seafood to succulent meat dishes and sweet treats, there is something for everyone. So be sure to pack your appetite and get ready to experience the culinary delights of the Greek Islands.

Greek Wine and Spirits

Greece is known for its ancient history, stunning beaches, and delicious cuisine, but it's also a country with a rich wine-making tradition. Greek wines have been enjoyed for thousands of years and are renowned for their distinctive flavors and aromas. If you're planning a trip to the Greek Islands, exploring the local wine and spirits is a must-do activity. In this chapter, we'll take a deep dive into the world of Greek wine and spirits, covering everything from the history of wine-making to the best places to sample local varieties.

Wine has been an important part of Greek culture since ancient times. The Greeks believed that wine was a gift from the gods and used it in religious ceremonies and as a medicinal remedy. The earliest evidence of wine-making in Greece dates back to 6,500 years ago, and the tradition has continued to evolve and thrive ever since.

Today, Greece has more than 300 indigenous grape varieties, many of which are not found anywhere else in the world. Some of the most well-known varieties include Agiorgitiko, Assyrtiko, Malagousia, Moschofilero, and

Xinomavro. Each grape variety has its own unique flavor profile, and Greek winemakers take great pride in showcasing the characteristics of their grapes in their wines.

Greek Wine Regions

There are several wine regions in Greece, each with its own distinct terroir and grape varieties. The most famous of these regions are Santorini, Crete, and the Peloponnese.

Santorini is known for its white wines made from the Assyrtiko grape, which grows in the island's volcanic soil. The resulting wine has a mineral-driven flavor profile with notes of citrus and stone fruit.

Crete is the largest of the Greek islands and is home to a diverse range of grape varieties. Some of the most popular wines from Crete are made from the Vidiano and Vilana grapes, which produce crisp, refreshing white wines.

The Peloponnese is a peninsula in southern Greece that is known for its red wines made from the Agiorgitiko grape. These wines have a rich, full-bodied flavor profile with notes of dark fruit and spice.

Greek Wine-Making Techniques

Greek winemakers use a range of techniques to produce their wines, from traditional methods that have been passed down through generations to more modern techniques that take advantage of new technology.

One of the most unique aspects of Greek wine-making is the use of amphorae, large clay vessels that are buried in the ground to ferment and age the wine. This method dates back to ancient times and is still used by some winemakers today.

Another important technique used by Greek winemakers is the use of skin contact. This involves leaving the grape skins in contact with the juice during fermentation, which results in wines with a fuller, more complex flavor profile.

Greek Spirits

In addition to wine, Greece is also known for its spirits. One of the most popular is ouzo, a clear, anise-flavored liquor that is typically served as an aperitif. Ouzo is made by distilling grape must and then adding anise and other botanicals.

Another popular Greek spirit is tsipouro, a grape-based spirit that is similar to Italian grappa. Tsipouro is typically served as a digestif and is often flavored with herbs such as mint or rosemary.

Things to Do and See

If you're interested in learning more about Greek wine and spirits, there are plenty of opportunities to do so while visiting the Greek Islands. Here are a few ideas:

Visit a winery: There are dozens of wineries throughout Greece that offer tours and tastings.

Attend a wine festival: Many towns and villages throughout Greece host wine festivals throughout the year. These events typically feature local wines, food, and live music.

Take a cooking class: Greek cuisine is known for its use of fresh ingredients and simple yet delicious flavors. Taking a cooking class that focuses on traditional Greek dishes is a great way to learn about the local food and wine culture.

Visit a distillery: In addition to wineries, there are also several distilleries throughout Greece that produce ouzo, tsipouro, and other spirits. Visiting a distillery is a great way to learn about the production process and sample the finished product.

Explore the local markets: Greek markets are a feast for the senses, with stalls selling everything from fresh produce and seafood to spices and honey. Exploring a local market is a great way to discover new flavors and ingredients to pair with your wine or spirits.

Exploring the world of Greek wine and spirits is an essential part of any trip to the Greek Islands. From the rich history of wine-making to the unique flavors and aromas of local varieties, there is something for everyone to discover. Whether you're a wine connoisseur or just looking to try something new, be sure to add a wine or spirits tasting to your itinerary. With so much to see and do, you're sure to leave with a new appreciation for the rich culture and traditions of Greece.

Chapter 8

Activities

As you plan your visit to the beautiful Greek Islands, one thing you'll quickly discover is that there's no shortage of activities to enjoy. From the stunning beaches to the charming villages and ancient ruins, there's something to appeal to every traveler's interests. Whether you're seeking relaxation or adventure, the islands offer an array of options to help you create the perfect itinerary for your trip.

In this guide, we'll explore some of the top activities you won't want to miss during your Greek Island getaway, so you can make the most of your time in this captivating corner of the world. So pack your bags, grab your camera, and get ready for an unforgettable experience in Greece.

Water Sports

When it comes to the Greek Islands, water sports are an essential part of any traveler's experience. From windsurfing and kitesurfing to kayaking and paddleboarding, there's something for everyone to enjoy in the crystal clear waters of the Aegean Sea.

If you're looking for an adrenaline rush, windsurfing and kitesurfing are great options. These sports are particularly popular on the islands of Naxos, Paros, and Rhodes, where the winds are strong and consistent. Experienced surfers can catch some serious air, while beginners can take lessons and learn the ropes from experienced instructors.

For those who prefer a more relaxing water activity, kayaking and paddleboarding are perfect choices. These sports are particularly popular on the islands of Crete and Corfu, where the calm waters allow for leisurely exploration of hidden coves and beaches. And for those who want to take their time and enjoy the scenery, a guided sea kayaking tour or SUP (stand-up paddleboarding) lesson can be a fantastic way to experience the beauty of the Greek Islands.

Scuba diving is also a great way to explore the underwater world of the Aegean Sea. Whether you're a beginner or an experienced diver, the Greek Islands offer some diving opportunities in the Mediterranean. From colorful reefs and underwater caves to ancient shipwrecks, there's something for everyone to discover beneath the waves.

And if you're looking for a truly unique water experience, why not try your hand at sea trekking? This innovative new activity allows you to explore the seafloor while wearing a special helmet that allows you to breathe underwater. It's a fantastic way to experience the beauty and wonder of the sea in a whole new way.

Of course, it's important to remember that water sports can be dangerous if proper precautions aren't taken. Always make sure to wear a life jacket or buoyancy aid, and never go out on the water alone. And if you're not a confident swimmer, consider taking swimming lessons or sticking to shallow waters where you can touch the bottom.

Overall, water sports are a fantastic way to experience the beauty and excitement of the Greek Islands. Whether you're looking for adventure, relaxation, or just a unique way to explore the sea, there's something for everyone to enjoy.

Windsurfing

This is one of the most popular water sports in the Greek Islands, and for good reason. With its perfect combination of wind, waves, and sunshine, Greece offers some of the best windsurfing conditions in the world.

The islands of Naxos, Paros, and Rhodes are particularly renowned for their windsurfing, with consistent winds and warm waters that are perfect for both beginners and advanced surfers. There are plenty of windsurfing schools and rental shops on these islands, making it easy to get started and explore the seas at your own pace.

For those who are new to the sport, taking a windsurfing lesson is a great way to learn the basics and get comfortable on the board. Experienced instructors will teach you how to read the wind and waves, how to control your speed and direction, and how to safely navigate the waters. With a bit of practice, you'll soon be gliding across the waves like a pro.

And for more experienced surfers, the Greek Islands offer plenty of challenging conditions that will put your skills to the test. From high winds and choppy seas to big waves and swells, there's always a new challenge to conquer and a new thrill to experience.

But perhaps the best thing about windsurfing in the Greek Islands is the stunning scenery. With its crystal-clear waters, rocky cliffs, and sandy beaches, Greece is a windsurfing paradise that offers endless opportunities for exploration and adventure. So whether you're a seasoned windsurfer or a complete beginner, there's no better place to experience the excitement and beauty of the sport than the Greek Islands.

Scuba Diving

Scuba diving is a popular activity in the Greek Islands, offering an opportunity to explore the rich underwater world of the Aegean Sea. With its clear waters, stunning reefs, and fascinating marine life, Greece is a top destination for scuba enthusiasts from around the world.

The Greek Islands offer a range of diving sites, from shallow reefs and rocky outcrops to deep caves and wrecks. Some of the most popular dive sites are located off the islands of Crete, Santorini, and Zakynthos, where you can explore ancient shipwrecks, colorful coral reefs, and stunning underwater rock formations.

For those who are new to scuba diving, there are plenty of diving schools and instructors in the Greek Islands who can provide training and certification. These courses will teach you the basics of scuba diving, including how to use the equipment, how to navigate underwater, and how to stay safe. Once you're certified, you'll be able to explore the underwater world on your own, with the guidance of experienced local divers.

One of the unique features of scuba diving in Greece is the abundance of ancient shipwrecks that lie beneath the waves. These wrecks offer a glimpse into the country's rich history and are a fascinating attraction for divers of all skill levels. Some of the most famous wrecks include the HMHS Britannic, which sank off the coast of Kea during World War I, and the Peristera shipwreck, which dates back to the 5th century BC.

But it's not just shipwrecks that make scuba diving in the Greek Islands so special. The underwater world is teeming with a variety of marine life, from colorful fish and sea turtles to octopuses and dolphins. And with its clear waters and excellent visibility, you'll be able to see everything in stunning detail.

Overall, scuba diving is an unforgettable experience in the Greek Islands. With its rich history, diverse marine life, and stunning underwater scenery, it's a must-do activity for anyone who loves to explore the natural world.

Sea kayaking

Sea kayaking is a popular activity among travelers visiting the Greek islands, and it is not difficult to understand why. With crystal clear waters, gorgeous coastlines, and stunning landscapes, there is no better way to explore the beauty of Greece's islands than from the seat of a kayak.

Kayaking is a perfect activity for those who enjoy the outdoors and appreciate being close to nature. It is an excellent way to experience the coastlines of the Greek islands, and you'll be rewarded with a unique perspective on the islands' beauty. Whether you're an experienced kayaker or a beginner, there are plenty of opportunities to enjoy this fantastic activity.

For those seeking a little adventure, sea kayaking is an excellent way to explore hidden coves, sea caves, and deserted beaches that can only be reached by sea. You'll be able to paddle your way through some of the most pristine waters in the world, enjoying views of crystal-clear waters teeming with marine life, and taking in the stunning scenery around you.

Kayaking is also a great way to get some exercise while on vacation. It's an excellent way to get your heart rate up and stay in shape while enjoying the beautiful outdoors. Plus, it's a low-impact exercise, making it perfect for travelers of all ages and fitness levels.

If you're interested in sea kayaking, there are plenty of opportunities to try it out while on the Greek islands. Many tour operators offer guided sea kayaking tours that take you to some of the most scenic spots around the islands. These tours often include all the necessary equipment, such as paddles, kayaks, and life jackets, and are led by experienced guides who will help you make the most of your kayaking adventure.

One of the best things about sea kayaking in the Greek islands is the variety of experiences available. You can choose to take a leisurely paddle around the coastline or challenge yourself with a more strenuous excursion. You can paddle through tranquil bays and inlets or ride the waves in the open sea. You can even try your hand at sea kayaking at night, which is an incredible experience that lets you see the islands in a completely different light.

Sea kayaking is also an excellent way to get to know the local culture and traditions of the Greek islands. You'll have the opportunity to interact with the locals, learn about their way of life, and even try some of their traditional foods. It's a great way to immerse yourself in the local culture and make lasting memories.

Finally, if you're interested in kayaking at home, you don't need to go all the way to Greece to enjoy this activity. Kayaking is a popular activity in many parts of the world, and there are plenty of opportunities to enjoy it wherever you live. From lakes and rivers to the open sea, kayaking is an amazing way to enjoy the natural beauty of your home region.

Sea kayaking is an excellent activity to include in your travel guide to the Greek islands. With its incredible natural beauty, unique cultural experiences, and diverse range of activities, kayaking is an activity that will appeal to travelers of all ages and interests. So whether you're a seasoned kayaker or a first-timer, be sure to add sea kayaking to your itinerary when visiting the Greek islands!

Hiking and Trekking

Hiking and trekking are two of the most popular outdoor activities in the Greek Islands. With rugged terrain, lush vegetation, and stunning views, the islands offer some of the best hiking and trekking trails in the world. Whether you're a seasoned hiker or a beginner, there are plenty of opportunities to explore the islands on foot and experience their natural beauty up close.

Hiking is a great way to explore the Greek Islands and get some exercise at the same time. With its rugged terrain and varied landscapes, there are trails for hikers of all levels, from easy strolls to challenging treks. You can hike through lush forests, across rocky peaks, and along breathtaking coastlines, taking in the stunning views and immersing yourself in the islands' natural beauty.

Trekking, on the other hand, is a more challenging and physically demanding activity that involves multi-day hikes and camping in the wilderness. The Greek Islands offer some of the best trekking opportunities in the world, with trails that take you through remote wilderness areas, past mountain lakes and rivers, and over high peaks and ridges.

Trekking in the Greek Islands is an unforgettable experience that lets you get up close and personal with the islands' rugged landscapes and natural beauty.

One of the best things about hiking and trekking in the Greek Islands is the incredible diversity of the trails available. You can hike through ancient forests, along rugged coastlines, or up steep mountains, each with unique challenges and rewards. You can choose a short hike or a multi-day trek, depending on your experience and fitness level. And with so many trails to choose from, you'll never run out of new places to explore.

Hiking and trekking in the Greek Islands is also a great way to connect with the local culture and traditions. You'll have the opportunity to interact with the locals, learn about their way of life, and even try some of their traditional foods. It's a great way to immerse yourself in the local culture and make lasting memories.

Finally, if you're interested in hiking and trekking at home, there are plenty of opportunities to enjoy these activities wherever you live. From local parks and trails to national parks and wilderness areas, there are trails for hikers of all levels and interests. Hiking and trekking are great ways to explore the natural beauty of your home region and get some exercise at the same time.

Hiking and trekking are two of the best ways to explore the natural beauty of the Greek Islands. With their rugged landscapes, diverse trails, and unique cultural experiences, hiking and trekking in the Greek Islands are activities that will appeal to travelers of all ages and interests.

Samaria Gorge

Samaria Gorge is a breathtaking destination that should be on every traveler's bucket list when visiting the Greek Islands. Located on the island of Crete, this natural wonder is a sight to behold, and exploring it is an unforgettable experience.

The Samaria Gorge is the longest gorge in Europe, stretching over 16 kilometers from the White Mountains to the Libyan Sea. The hike through the gorge is an activity that will undoubtedly take your breath away, both literally and figuratively. The trek starts at the Omalos plateau and winds its way down the rocky terrain, leading you through a narrow pathway that's surrounded by towering limestone walls. As you descend, the landscape changes, and you'll find yourself surrounded by pine and cypress trees, wildflowers, and the sweet aroma of herbs like thyme and oregano.

The journey through the gorge takes around five to seven hours, depending on your pace, and can be challenging, so make sure you're wearing comfortable shoes and carrying plenty of water and snacks. But the reward for your efforts is worth it – the views along the way are spectacular, and the feeling of accomplishment at the end of the hike is unmatched.

As you make your way through the Samaria Gorge, you'll come across several landmarks that add to the charm of the place. The Iron Gates, for example, is a narrow passage where the walls of the gorge are just four meters apart, and the only way forward is through the riverbed. It's an exhilarating experience to wade through the cool waters, with the cliffs towering above you on either side.

Another highlight of the Samaria Gorge is the village of Samaria, which is located near the end of the trek. The village was abandoned in the 1960s when the gorge was turned into a national park, but a few families have returned to make it their home. Walking through the village is like taking a step back in time – the traditional stone houses and the sound of sheep bells in the distance make for a charming experience.

The Samaria Gorge is not just a destination for nature lovers; it's also a great place for history buffs. The gorge has played an important role in the region's history, serving as a route for rebels during the Cretan War of Independence in the 19th century. The remnants of the rebel hideouts can still be seen along the trek, adding an extra layer of intrigue to the experience.

A visit to the Samaria Gorge is an activity that should not be missed when exploring the Greek Islands. It's a perfect example of the stunning natural beauty that the region has to offer, and the trek through the gorge is an adventure that will stay with you for a lifetime. Whether you're a seasoned hiker or just looking for a unique experience, the Samaria Gorge is a must-visit destination that you won't regret adding to your itinerary.

Mount Olympus

Mount Olympus is an awe-inspiring mountain that stands majestically in Greece, and it is one of the most iconic mountains in the world. This magnificent peak is located in the heart of Thessaly and is surrounded by stunning Greek islands. It is a place that many people dream of visiting, and it is easy to see why.

Mount Olympus is a place of myths and legends, and it is the highest mountain in Greece, standing at 2,917 meters (9,570 feet) tall. It is said to be the home of the gods in Greek mythology, and it is believed that Zeus, the king of gods, lived on the summit of the mountain. The ancient Greeks believed that the gods held their council on the mountain, and that it was a place of great power and divine energy.

Today, Mount Olympus is an attraction for hikers, climbers, and adventurers from different countries. The mountain offers a variety of activities that are perfect for travelers looking for an adventure. The trails leading up to the summit are well-marked and offer breathtaking views of the surrounding islands and coastline.

Hiking is one of the most popular activities on Mount Olympus, and there are several trails to choose from, each with unique challenges and rewards. The most popular route is the E4 trail, which starts in Litochoro and takes hikers through stunning forests and rocky terrain before reaching the summit.

Another popular activity on Mount Olympus is rock climbing. The mountain offers a variety of routes for climbers of all skill levels, and it is a great way to experience the mountain's natural beauty up close. Climbers can choose to climb the rocky cliffs or explore the mountain's caves and gorges.

For those who prefer a more relaxed pace, Mount Olympus also offers a range of other activities. Visitors can enjoy horse riding, mountain biking, or simply take a leisurely stroll through the mountain's beautiful forests and valleys.

If you're looking for an unforgettable experience, why not spend a night on the mountain? There are several mountain refuges on Mount Olympus that offer hikers and climbers a place to rest and refuel. Spending the night on the mountain is a unique experience, and it offers a chance to experience the mountain's magic in a whole new way.

Mount Olympus is a must-be destination for visitors to the Greek islands. It is a place of beauty, adventure, and mythology, and it offers something for everyone. Whether you're an experienced hiker, a seasoned climber, or just looking for a relaxing escape, Mount Olympus is a place you won't want to miss. So pack your bags, and get ready for the adventure of a lifetime!

The Corfu Trail

The Corfu Trail is one of the most scenic and rewarding hiking trails in Greece, offering a unique perspective on the beautiful island of Corfu. This trail takes hikers on a journey through picturesque villages, lush forests, olive groves, and rocky coastlines, providing a glimpse into the island's rich culture and natural beauty.

The Corfu Trail is approximately 220 kilometers long and covers the length of the island from the southernmost tip to the northernmost point. The trail is divided into 10 sections, each with its own unique challenges and rewards. Hikers can choose to hike the entire trail or pick and choose specific sections based on their interests and abilities.

The trail starts in the traditional village of Kavos in the south and leads hikers through quaint villages like Lefkimmi and Spartera. Along the way, hikers will encounter ancient ruins, including the remains of a Roman villa in the village of Agioi Deka. The trail also offers stunning views of the island's rugged coastline, with secluded beaches.

As hikers venture further north, they will encounter the island's stunning mountain range, where they can enjoy panoramic views of the island. The trail leads through the dense forests of Mount Pantokrator, the highest peak on the island, and offers hikers the opportunity to see rare plant and animal species.

One of the highlights of the Corfu Trail is the chance to experience the island's unique culture and history. Hikers can visit traditional villages and taste local cuisine, including the island's famous olive oil, wine, and fresh seafood. Along the way, hikers will also encounter ancient churches and monasteries, each with its own unique story and significance.

The Corfu Trail is a challenging but rewarding experience, and hikers should be prepared with sturdy footwear, plenty of water, and sunscreen. However, the trail is accessible to hikers of all levels, with well-marked paths and plenty of opportunities to rest and refuel.

The Corfu Trail is a must-visit destination for hikers and nature lovers visiting Greece. It offers a unique and authentic experience of the island's natural beauty and cultural heritage, and it is an adventure that is not to be missed. Whether you're an experienced hiker or a casual nature enthusiast, the Corfu Trail is an unforgettable journey that will leave you with memories to last a lifetime.

Nightlife

Nightlife is an essential aspect of any travel experience, and the Greek islands are no exception. The nightlife scene in Greece is vibrant, exciting, and offers something for everyone, whether you're looking for a quiet night out or an all-night party.

One of the most popular nightlife destinations in Greece is Mykonos. This island is famous for its glamorous party scene, with a host of beach clubs, bars, and nightclubs catering to a stylish and sophisticated crowd. Some of the most popular nightlife spots on the island include Cavo Paradiso, which offers stunning views of the sea and hosts world-famous DJs, and Jackie O', a stylish beach club that is perfect for sunset cocktails and dancing under the stars.

Santorini is another island that offers a unique and unforgettable nightlife experience. The island is famous for its beautiful sunsets, and many bars and restaurants offer stunning views of the sunset over the Aegean Sea. Some of the most popular nightlife spots on the island include Koo Club, a lively bar and nightclub that attracts a young and trendy crowd, and Tango Bar, a sophisticated and elegant spot that offers live music and dancing.

For those looking for a more laid-back and traditional nightlife experience, the island of Crete is a great option. The island is home to many small villages and towns.

Visitors can enjoy a traditional meal at a taverna, listen to live music at a local bar, or simply stroll through the narrow streets and soak up the atmosphere.

Another great option for nightlife is Rhodes, which is home to a vibrant and varied nightlife scene. Visitors can enjoy live music and dancing at one of the island's many nightclubs, or relax with a cocktail at a beachfront bar. Some of the most popular nightlife spots on the island include Paradiso Beach Club, which offers live DJs and a lively atmosphere, and Colorado Club, a cozy bar with a laid-back vibe.

The Greek islands offer a diverse and exciting nightlife scene, with something for everyone. Whether you're looking for a glamorous party scene or a traditional and laid-back experience, the Greek islands have it all. So, get ready to dance the night away, sip cocktails under the stars, and experience the unforgettable nightlife of the Greek islands.

Bars and Clubs

Bars and clubs are an essential part of the nightlife scene on the Greek islands, offering visitors the opportunity to experience the local culture and socialize with other travelers. Each island has its own unique atmosphere and character, and there are countless options to choose from when it comes to bars and clubs.

Mykonos is known as the party island of Greece, and it's no surprise that it's home to some of the best bars and clubs in the country. The island is famous for its lively beach parties, and visitors can dance the night away at one of the many beach clubs, such as Scorpios, which offers an open-air dance floor and breathtaking views of the sea. For those looking for a more intimate atmosphere, the Little Venice area of Mykonos town is home to many cozy bars and restaurants, such as the popular Caprice Bar, which offers live music and a laid-back vibe.

Santorini is another island that boasts a vibrant nightlife scene, with a variety of bars and clubs to choose from. The island is famous for its sunset views, and many bars offer stunning views of the sunset over the Aegean Sea. One of the most popular bars on the island is Franco's Bar, which is located on the edge of the caldera and offers spectacular views of the sea and volcano. For those looking for a more lively atmosphere, Koo Club is a popular nightclub that attracts a young and trendy crowd.

If you're looking for a more traditional Greek island experience, head to the island of Crete, which is home to many charming villages and towns with cozy bars and tavernas. The town of Chania, for example, is home to many traditional bars and cafes, where visitors can enjoy a local drink and soak up the atmosphere. For those looking for a more modern nightlife experience, the town of Malia is home to many lively bars and clubs, such as Candy Club, which offers live DJs and a bustling dance floor.

Rhodes is another island that boasts a diverse and exciting nightlife scene. The town of Rhodes is home to many lively bars and nightclubs, such as the popular Club Inferno, which is located in a medieval building and offers a unique atmosphere. For those looking for a more relaxed atmosphere, Lindos is a charming village with many cozy bars and restaurants, such as the rooftop bar at Melenos Lindos Hotel, which offers stunning views of the sea.

The Greek islands offer a wide range of options when it comes to bars and clubs, with something for everyone. Whether you're looking for a glamorous party scene or a traditional and laid-back experience, the Greek islands have it all.

Open-air Cinemas

Open-air cinemas are a unique and charming feature of the Greek islands' cultural landscape. These outdoor cinemas offer visitors the opportunity to enjoy a film under the stars. The experience is one that is not to be missed, and many travelers consider it a highlight of their trip to Greece.

One of the most famous open-air cinemas in Greece is Cine Kamari on the island of Santorini. This cinema is located in the picturesque village of Kamari, and visitors can enjoy a movie while taking in the stunning views of the Aegean Sea. The cinema also has a restaurant and bar, it is a perfect spot to relax after a long day of exploring the island.

Another popular open-air cinema is Cine Manto on the island of Mykonos. This cinema is located in a beautiful garden in Mykonos town and offers a unique and intimate atmosphere. Visitors can enjoy a film while surrounded by the lush greenery of the garden, making for a magical and unforgettable experience.

The island of Paros is also home to a popular open-air cinema called Cine Rex. This cinema is located in the heart of Parikia, the island's main town, and offers a cozy and welcoming atmosphere. Visitors can enjoy a film while sipping on a refreshing drink or enjoying a traditional Greek snack.

If you're visiting the island of Crete, be sure to check out the open-air cinema in the town of Chania. This cinema is located in a charming courtyard in the heart of the town, and visitors can enjoy a film while surrounded by the beautiful architecture and historical landmarks of the town.

Open-air cinemas are a unique and magical experience that should not be missed when visiting the Greek islands.

Traditional Greek Entertainment

When it comes to traditional Greek entertainment, there is a rich and diverse cultural landscape to explore. From music and dance to theater and storytelling, the Greek islands offer visitors a chance to experience the unique and vibrant traditions of Greece.

One of the most popular forms of traditional Greek entertainment is live music. Visitors can enjoy a variety of traditional Greek music styles, including rebetiko, which originated in the early 20th century and is often described as the Greek blues. Many bars and tavernas on the Greek islands offer live music performances, and visitors can enjoy a night of music and dancing while soaking up the local culture.

Another popular form of traditional Greek entertainment is folk dance. The islands of Greece have a rich history of dance, and visitors can experience a variety of styles, including the famous Syrtaki, which is often associated with the movie "Zorba the Greek". Many villages and towns on the Greek islands hold traditional dance festivals throughout the summer months, where visitors can watch or even participate in the dancing.

The theater is also an important part of Greek culture, and visitors can experience traditional Greek theater performances in many of the island's historic theaters. One of the most famous theaters is the ancient theater of Epidaurus, located on the Peloponnese Peninsula, which dates back to the 4th century BC and is still used for performances today.

For those interested in storytelling, the Greek islands offer a rich tradition of oral storytelling and poetry. Many cafes and tavernas on the islands host storytelling nights, where visitors can listen to local storytellers recount traditional Greek myths and legends.

Traditional Greek entertainment offers visitors a unique and fascinating glimpse into the rich cultural history of Greece. Whether you're interested in music, dance, theater, or storytelling, there is something for everyone to enjoy on the Greek islands. So, sit back, relax, and immerse yourself in the captivating world of traditional Greek entertainment.

Chapter 8

Practical Information

Exploring the stunning Greek Islands is a dream come true for many travelers. From the pristine beaches to the historic landmarks, there's no shortage of beauty and culture to discover. But before you set off on your adventure, it's important to have practical information at your fingertips. Knowing the best time to visit, what to pack, how to get around, and where to stay can make all the difference in creating a smooth and stress-free vacation.

Below is practical information you need to make the most of your trip and create unforgettable memories.

Language

Language is an essential part of any travel experience, and being prepared with some basic knowledge of the local language can greatly enhance your trip to the Greek Islands. Greek is the official language of Greece and is spoken by the majority of the population, with various dialects found on different islands. While many Greeks speak English, it is always appreciated when visitors attempt to speak Greek, and it can make a significant difference in your interactions with locals.

One of the first things you should learn is how to say hello and goodbye. In Greek, "hello" is "yassou" (pronounced yah-soo), and "goodbye" is "yia sou" (pronounced yah-soo). Other basic phrases that can come in handy include "please" (parakalo), "thank you" (efharisto), "yes" (ne), and "no" (ochi).

Knowing some basic phrases can be especially useful in restaurants and shops. For example, "the bill, please" is "to logariasmo, parakalo" (pronounced toh loh-gah-ree-ahs-moh, pah-rah-kah-loh), while "how much does this cost?" is "poso kani afto?" (pronounced poh-soh kah-nee ahf-toh).

It is also important to familiarize yourself with the Greek alphabet, as it differs from the Latin alphabet used in English. For example, the Greek letter alpha (α) is pronounced "ah," while beta (β) is pronounced "v." Learning the Greek alphabet can help you read signs, menus, and other written materials.

While Greek is the official language of Greece, it's worth noting that many island communities have their own dialects and regional differences in pronunciation and vocabulary. For example, the dialect spoken on the island of Crete is known for its distinctive accent and vocabulary. It's always a good idea to ask locals if they have any specific phrases or words they use in their community.

When it comes to navigating daily life on the Greek Islands, knowing some language basics can help you feel more at home. For example, "where is the nearest pharmacy?" is "pou einai i kontinotera farmakeio?" (pronounced poo eh-nai ee kohn-tee-noh-teh-rah fahr-mah-kee-oh), while "where can I find a taxi?" is "pou boroh na vro ena taksi?" (pronounced poo boh-roh nah vroh eh-nah tahk-see).

In summary, learning some basic Greek phrases and becoming familiar with the Greek alphabet can greatly enhance your travel experience on the Greek Islands. Don't be afraid to practice your Greek with locals - they will appreciate the effort and may even offer to teach you more!

Currency

When traveling to the Greek Islands, it's important to be aware of the local currency and exchange rates. The official currency of Greece is the Euro, which is used across the country and its islands. The Euro is divided into 100 cents, with coins available in denominations of 1, 2, 5, 10, 20, and

50 cents, as well as 1 and 2 Euro coins. Banknotes come in denominations of 5, 10, 20, 50, 100, 200, and 500 Euros.

It's a good idea to exchange some currency before your trip to have some cash on hand, especially if you plan to visit smaller islands or rural areas where credit cards may not be accepted. ATMs are widely available on larger islands and in major towns and cities, but it's a good idea to check with your bank about any fees or charges for using international ATMs.

When exchanging money, be sure to compare rates and fees between banks and currency exchange bureaus to ensure you get the best value. Some businesses may also accept other currencies, such as US dollars or British pounds, but be aware that the exchange rate may not be favorable.

Credit cards are widely accepted in larger cities and tourist areas, but it's always a good idea to carry some cash for smaller transactions and to be prepared in case of any issues with card payments. It's also worth noting that some businesses may charge a fee for credit card transactions, so it's best to ask before making a purchase.

Overall, it's important to be aware of the local currency and exchange rates when traveling to the Greek Islands to ensure a smooth and stress-free trip. With some planning and preparation, you can enjoy your travels and make the most of your time on these beautiful islands.

Safety

Safety is a key concern for any traveler, and the Greek Islands are no exception. While the islands are generally considered safe for visitors, it's always a good idea to take some basic precautions to ensure a safe and enjoyable trip.

One of the main safety concerns on the Greek Islands is pickpocketing and theft, particularly in crowded tourist areas and on public transport. It's important to keep your valuables, such as cash, passports, and electronics, secure and out of sight. Be aware of your surroundings and avoid carrying large amounts of cash or wearing expensive jewelry.

Another safety concern on the Greek Islands is the risk of sunburn and heat exhaustion, particularly during the summer months. Be sure to wear sunscreen, a hat, and light clothing to protect your skin from the sun, and stay hydrated by drinking plenty of water throughout the day.

If you plan to swim in the sea, be aware of any warnings or advisories about strong currents or jellyfish. Always swim in designated areas and be cautious of any sudden changes in weather or sea conditions.

In terms of transportation, it's important to exercise caution when driving or riding mopeds or motorcycles. The roads on some islands can be narrow and winding, and local drivers may have different driving habits than what you're used to. Wear a helmet if you're riding a moped or motorcycle, and always use a seatbelt if you're driving or riding in a car.

It's also a good idea to familiarize yourself with the emergency phone number in Greece, which is 112. This number can be used for any type of emergency, including medical, police, or fire.

Overall, with some basic precautions and common sense, the Greek Islands can be a safe and enjoyable travel destination. By staying aware of your surroundings and taking care of yourself, you can make the most of your trip and create lasting memories.

Health

Maintaining good health is important when traveling to the Greek Islands. Here are some tips to help you stay healthy and enjoy your trip:

Stay hydrated: The Greek Islands can get hot and humid during the summer months, so it's important to drink plenty of water to avoid dehydration. Carry a water bottle with you at all times and drink water regularly throughout the day.

Protect yourself from the sun: Sunburn can be a major health concern when visiting the Greek Islands, especially if you plan to spend a lot of time outdoors. Wear a hat, sunglasses, and sunscreen with a high SPF rating to protect your skin from the sun.

Be careful with food and water: While the tap water in the Greek Islands is generally safe to drink, it's still a good idea to stick to bottled water, especially if you have a sensitive stomach. Be careful with street food and ensure that any meat or seafood is cooked thoroughly before eating.

Take precautions against mosquitoes: Mosquitoes can be a problem in some areas of the Greek Islands, especially during the summer months. Wear long-sleeved clothing and use mosquito repellent to avoid bites.

Be prepared for emergencies: It's a good idea to pack a basic first aid kit with items such as bandages, antiseptic cream, and painkillers. Make sure you have adequate travel insurance and familiarize yourself with the location of the nearest medical facilities.

Exercise caution when swimming: The waters around the Greek Islands can be treacherous, with strong currents and unpredictable weather conditions. Always swim in designated areas and be aware of any warnings or advisories about jellyfish or other sea creatures.

By following these tips and taking care of your health, you can enjoy your trip to the Greek Islands and create unforgettable memories.

Tipping

Tipping is not mandatory in the Greek Islands, but it is appreciated for good service. Here are some guidelines to help you navigate the tipping culture in Greece:

Restaurants: It's customary to leave a small tip of around 5-10% of the total bill if you're satisfied with the service. Some restaurants may include a service charge on the bill, so be sure to check before tipping.

Bars: If you're just ordering drinks at a bar, it's not necessary to leave a tip. However, if you're sitting at a table and receiving table service, a small tip of around 5% is appreciated.

Taxis: Tipping taxi drivers is not expected, but rounding up the fare to the nearest euro is a common practice.

Hotels: It's customary to tip hotel staff, such as housekeeping and bellhops, a small amount of around 1-2 euros per day. If you receive exceptional service from the hotel staff, you may choose to leave a larger tip.

Tour guides: If you take a guided tour, it's common to tip the guide at the end of the tour. A tip of around 5-10 euros per person is appropriate for a half-day tour, while a full-day tour may warrant a larger tip of around 10-20 euros per person.

Remember, tipping is optional, and you should only tip if you feel that the service you received warrants it. It's always a good idea to carry some small bills or coins with you for tipping purposes, as not all establishments may accept credit cards for tips.

Conclusion

The Greek Islands are a place of wonder, with their sun-drenched beaches, crystal-clear waters, and rich cultural heritage. For centuries, this archipelago has drawn travelers from around the world Join us on a journey through the Greek Islands, exploring their hidden gems and must-see attractions.

From the white-washed villages of Santorini to the rugged mountains of Crete, this guide is your passport to an unforgettable adventure. Discover the ancient temples of Delos, walk in the footsteps of the Minoans, and soak up the vibrant atmosphere of Mykonos.

But this guide isn't just about sightseeing. We'll also introduce you to the local cuisine, help you navigate the islands' bustling markets, and offer insider tips on the best beaches and hiking trails. And if you're looking for a more immersive experience, we'll even show you how to volunteer with local organizations and support sustainable tourism.

So, whether you're planning a family vacation, a romantic getaway, or a solo adventure, this guide is your ultimate companion to the Greek Islands. With its comprehensive coverage, expert recommendations, and stunning photography, it's sure to inspire you to explore every corner of this magical destination. Get ready to fall in love with the Greek Islands - the adventure of a lifetime awaits!

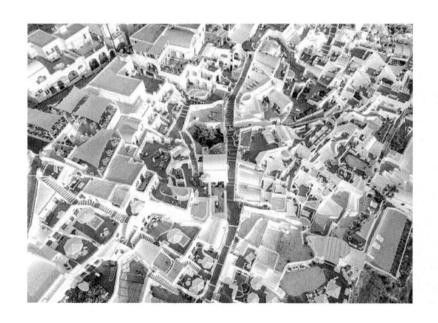

TRAVEL PLANNERS

TRAVEL

DATE:

DURATION:

DESTINATION:

PLACES TO SEE:	LOCAL FOOD TO TRY:
1	1
2	2
3	3
4	4
5	5
6	6
7	7

DAY 1	DAY 2	DAY 3

DAY 4	DAY 5	DAY 6

NOTES	EXPENSES IN TOTAL:

PLANNER

TRAVEL

DATE:

DURATION:

DESTINATION:

PLACES TO SEE:	LOCAL FOOD TO TRY:
1	1
2	2
3	3
4	4
5	5
6	6
7	7

DAY 1	DAY 2	DAY 3

DAY 4	DAY 5	DAY 6

NOTES	EXPENSES IN TOTAL:

PLANNER

TRAVEL

DATE:

DURATION:

DESTINATION:

PLACES TO SEE:	LOCAL FOOD TO TRY:
1 _____	1 _____
2 _____	2 _____
3 _____	3 _____
4 _____	4 _____
5 _____	5 _____
6 _____	6 _____
7 _____	7 _____

DAY 1	DAY 2	DAY 3

DAY 4	DAY 5	DAY 6

NOTES	EXPENSES IN TOTAL:

PLANNER

TRAVEL

DATE:

DURATION:

DESTINATION:

PLACES TO SEE:	LOCAL FOOD TO TRY:
1 _____	1 _____
2 _____	2 _____
3 _____	3 _____
4 _____	4 _____
5 _____	5 _____
6 _____	6 _____
7 _____	7 _____

DAY 1	DAY 2	DAY 3

DAY 4	DAY 5	DAY 6

NOTES	EXPENSES IN TOTAL:

PLANNER

TRAVEL

DATE:

DURATION:

DESTINATION:

PLACES TO SEE:	LOCAL FOOD TO TRY:

PLACES TO SEE:
1 _____
2 _____
3 _____
4 _____
5 _____
6 _____
7 _____

LOCAL FOOD TO TRY:
1 _____
2 _____
3 _____
4 _____
5 _____
6 _____
7 _____

DAY 1	DAY 2	DAY 3

DAY 4	DAY 5	DAY 6

NOTES	EXPENSES IN TOTAL:

PLANNER

TRAVEL

DATE:

DURATION:

DESTINATION:

PLACES TO SEE:	LOCAL FOOD TO TRY:
1	1
2	2
3	3
4	4
5	5
6	6
7	7

DAY 1	DAY 2	DAY 3

DAY 4	DAY 5	DAY 6

NOTES	EXPENSES IN TOTAL:

PLANNER

TRAVEL

DATE:

DURATION:

DESTINATION:

PLACES TO SEE:	LOCAL FOOD TO TRY:
1	1
2	2
3	3
4	4
5	5
6	6
7	7

DAY 1	DAY 2	DAY 3

DAY 4	DAY 5	DAY 6

NOTES	EXPENSES IN TOTAL:

PLANNER

TRAVEL

DATE:

DURATION:

DESTINATION:

PLACES TO SEE:	LOCAL FOOD TO TRY:
1 _____	1 _____
2 _____	2 _____
3 _____	3 _____
4 _____	4 _____
5 _____	5 _____
6 _____	6 _____
7 _____	7 _____

DAY 1	DAY 2	DAY 3

DAY 4	DAY 5	DAY 6

NOTES	EXPENSES IN TOTAL:

PLANNER

TRAVEL

DATE:

DURATION:

DESTINATION:

PLACES TO SEE:	LOCAL FOOD TO TRY:
1 _____	1 _____
2 _____	2 _____
3 _____	3 _____
4 _____	4 _____
5 _____	5 _____
6 _____	6 _____
7 _____	7 _____

DAY 1	DAY 2	DAY 3

DAY 4	DAY 5	DAY 6

NOTES	EXPENSES IN TOTAL:

PLANNER

TRAVEL

DATE:

DURATION:

DESTINATION:

PLACES TO SEE:	LOCAL FOOD TO TRY:
1 _____	1 _____
2 _____	2 _____
3 _____	3 _____
4 _____	4 _____
5 _____	5 _____
6 _____	6 _____
7 _____	7 _____

DAY 1	DAY 2	DAY 3

DAY 4	DAY 5	DAY 6

NOTES	EXPENSES IN TOTAL:

PLANNER

Printed in Great Britain
by Amazon

23305504R00099